The Nutmeg Anthology
Contemporary Poems of Connecticut

The Nutmeg Anthology
Contemporary Poems of Connecticut

✳✳✳

Edited by Ginny Lowe Connors

GRAYSON BOOKS
West Hartford, Connecticut
graysonbooks.com

The Nutmeg Anthology: Contemporary Poems of Connecticut
Copyright © 2026 Ginny Lowe Connors
Published by Grayson Books
West Hartford, Connecticut
ISBN: 979-8-9985883-4-1
Library of Congress Control Number: 2026930020

Cover Image: © Diana Lee Angstadt Photography, www.diana-angstadt.pixels.com
Book and Cover Design: Cindy Stewart

Contents

In All Weathers

Introduction

You can't generalize about Connecticut, because Bridgeport is always ready to unsettle what you might say about Bridgewater. Bishop's Orchards isn't the Buckland Hills Mall, and Jonathan Trumbull isn't Geno Auriemma, even if they both gave rise to state dynasties. Connecticut is named in the language of people who have lived here since time immemorial, and one in six of its residents today is an immigrant.

Thankfully, this anthology invites us to ignore the problem of generalizations. Instead, the poems assembled here give us the gift of particulars. Here are Pratt & Whitney, Pepe's Pizza, Weir Farm, and the witch trials. Here are Elizabeth Park, Yale-New Haven Hospital, Wallace Stevens, the Pequot Massacre, the Sandy Hook shooting, IKEA, the Hartford Circus Fire, Mark Twain, Louis Kahn, the New Britain Museum of Art, the Raymond Library, the Greater Hartford Twilight League, the Colt Factory, Florence Griswold, Cumberland Farms, and those citizens of Allingtown who have never acquiesced to being part of West Haven.

Let me reassure you that the experience of reading these poems is much less chaotic than that list might suggest. Maybe it was the general grace of the work, or maybe it was the happy encounter with the uncorrupted spirit of anyone who understands why it is worth writing a poem in the twenty-first century United States, but I didn't find the anthology discordant at all. I found this book comforting. When I thought about why, I realized, it's because it felt like home.

—Andy Horowitz, Connecticut State Historian

In the Neighborhood

Melissa Dione McEwen

Sketch of Albany Ave. in the Afternoon, Late January

Bodega prayer candles
altar the sidewalk.

Neighborhood boys
a street corner congregation.

Rush hour traffic
a slow-moving inner-city parade

of people in vehicles
trying to get to suburban homes

after working all day long
in insurance buildings downtown.

The city buses
are floats.

Right now, at this very moment,
the sky is flamingo pink

and a cloud high above Citgo
kind of looks like Jesus.

John Long

Hungerford Street

Hartford, Connecticut, 1975

February in a heat wave sounds like spring.
I hear thawing surround me as I walk,
one roof has a single drip ringing loud,
each drop hits an empty beer can in the lawn.

Another house, melting snow pours off the eave,
like a steady rain slapping the sidewalk.
At noon the carillon at the corner church plays
Lutheran hymns of faith and joy.

Children with rubber boots high step through
every puddle, jump into the biggest ones,
making as much water noise as they can
delighted with each splash and squish sound.

With the muted roar of a tiny avalanche, snow
scrapes over roof shingles to splatter
the sidewalk, the children screech and run,
I'm marooned on high ground with no boots.

I walk, avoiding puddles like a drunk
trying to dance to music no one else hears.
Water gurgles and circles the drain, then plunges
into the dark echoes of metal pipes.

After three blocks, salsa blares from open windows
of the rooms above the bodega that was a deli.
I hear the announcer shout, "Bailemos, bailemos"
as the drums and horns begin the next song.

Men speaking many languages laugh out loud
happily together, standing on the corner,
their corner, to pass the brown bag,
fruity wine to honor early spring.

Bessy Reyna

Lunch Walk in Hartford

He came bouncing down the street,
heavy body, long hair, jacket and tie.
There was an oddness about him.
Then, as he approached
I heard the sound of maracas
coming from his pockets.

Was it candy?
I pictured hundreds of multi-colored sweets
crashing against each other,
he, oblivious to the crackling rhythm.

Along Capitol Avenue
our paths crossed,
lunch break nearly over.

How can I explain
being late for work
because I was following a man
who sounded like maracas?

Dennis Barone

In the Public Garden

It is our oasis in this suburb,
shrine to a thought provided shape.
It whispers to us,
something about mutability in an age of steel,
an answer to desire unfilled.

Sherri Bedingfield

Conversation with White Rose

Elizabeth Park, Hartford, Connecticut

It's morning, you and I are here with early feeders
next to a lake with silver carp and brown sunnys.
Carpenter bees, robins, grackles, a dove,
and great crow at her distance.
You and I, white rose, are anything but drowsy.

The sky's light turns your petals lavender blue
like a famous celebrity's eyes.
I imagine you in a raised garden, edged with trimmed
grass and women of different ages seated at a stone table
in metal chairs, having tea and serious conversation.

I remember a friend's mother I felt close to.
Her tender hands, velvet brown eyes, she wore your color
and wanted me to wear it instead of my black tee shirt.
Other roses surround us. Pinks, my favorite, and garnet red.
Amber Flush, a yellow. And tender lavender.

Today their necks lift skyward like yours. The cycle of winter
softens to spring. Your roots thicken and push down through
earth again, a dormant death becomes another birth.

Elaine Zimmerman

The Guest

Bear comes to the party uninvited.
He likes the look of the cupcakes.
A child shrieks, bear sniffing the red
shirt buttons up and down her spine.
Toddlers are swept inside, positioned
at bay windows in the kitchen, peering
out. Bear slowly licks the tops off each
cupcake, strawberry icing to his liking.
Then chomps the vanilla cake bottoms
in one quick bite, green paper and all.
The children delight in his reckless
manner and style. Enormity of one gulp.
How much fits in a single paw. Lolling
about, he reaches, scratches, pushes
cups and plates loudly out of the way.
The birthday boy is pleased and confused.
Laughter, fear and some kind of sadness
mix together like a messy floor puzzle.
Where are the piled-high presents, next
to striped blue gift bags for each friend?
Fat pinata hangs off the old oak, ribbons
dangling low and soon to be clawed.
It's like being at the city zoo for his party.
But bear is alone outside with treats and
shiny hats. They're all inside, staring out.

Sharon Smith

Whose Woods

for my neighborhood's biggest black bear

He saunters by on solid, low-slung
haunches, sniffs at our grill
continues on his way unimpressed
by our landscaping efforts.

He doesn't give one damn
about deeds or rights-of-way.

He lives in these woods
was born in these woods.
He will walk where he pleases.
He will eat what he finds.

His kin predated these condos.

I watch from my window,
impressed by his smooth-muscled
glide, thick black coat
his calm, cool countenance.

I don't take a picture. It would feel petty.

He crosses the street
picks my neighbors' biggest pumpkin
up in his teeth, swings it back and forth
slowly by its stem and walks unhurriedly
back into these woods we share.

But really   he owns.

Julia Meylor Simpsom

For Those Who Must

For the staff at the Lyman Allyn Art Museum,
New London, Connecticut

I have watched an artist hang her canvases
with breathless care—unswaddling her work
like infants from family quilts—but who attended
her own opening with reluctant dread.

I have listened to daughters tell stories
of their artist mother, whose paintings once hung
in their childhood home, and how they cried
upon seeing her art on a gallery wall for the first time.

I have gazed through a magnifying glass
to focus on ink strokes as fine as cilia
in miniatures painted by eighteenth century sisters,
one of whom went blind after years of plying her trade.

I have interrogated a roomful of abstracts
that smash and trash and rehash
boxed conventions of beauty and truth
while standing in awe of countless hues of blue.

I have searched newsclips about a 22-year-old artist
who jumped off a train in New London,
where she gave drawing lessons to the city's children
and collected their coins to feed her passion.

I, too, have tasted an artist's need to create—
it is the dark pit that sprouts into tender vines
despite row upon row of infertile fields.
It is the must that burdens us—and unburdens us.

Mark McGuire-Schwartz

You can tell your story, and I'll tell mine

Impressions of Art at the New Britain Museum of American Art

1

I have sat at that table.

2

I have been that boy.

3

I do not remember the hunger,
but I remember being there.

4

I am Avery's daughter at the beach.

5

What a bright and happy
painter you were, John
Himmelfarb, until I read
the wall plaque explaining
your painting.

6

It seems that the red that
gave me such joy is really blood.
And that the black represents
menacing figures,
soldiers who have shot
Mr. Red, and may shoot him
again.

7
Lee Krasner, when you were 30
you painted the still life: still
visible is the banana, the guitar.

8
Lee, the banana was there before
you met Jackson Pollack, before you married
Jackson Pollack, before Jackson Pollack became famous,
before he had killed anyone.

9
Adolf Gottlieb, your Omen for Huts . . .

10
Tiger, you were in my dream.

11
In 1932, there was light on shoulders,
and we all had paunch
and bones.

12
Thomas Hart Benton,
how you see us. Music is a key.
But there are guns and horses
and a buffalo, too. You see America
playing, just as Whitman heard America sing.
And we pray.

13
I am the boy. The one with the face.
I am the mother, green
with spoon. But not the
chair. Not the aunt.

14
The wind is blowing
and a woman is crying.
and she is saying,
"Mom got me all upset."

15
Calder, with your
red and black.

16
I sit on a bear
and he is bronze
and lets me. I pat his
head, and stroke his smooth
ears.

17
Bear, I befriend you.
I will name you in my will.
I will sit with you for a while.

Kevin Carey

Some Might Call It Insomnia

Little mill town, the poorest in the valley,
trying hard to be more, than football.
Big Blue Chargers decades of success,
outstripping the comfort of the last century.
At Nolan Field you can hear the crowd
rumble like the train that links Waterbury
to Bridgeport—a world behind the concrete
wall built to protect, insulate, after Connie,
then Diane devastated buildings, washed wooden
bridges, people, possessions away—downstream.

It's a brash blue-collar pride, bold,
unapologetic confidence, that quietly knows politics
is—personal, based on decades of relationships.
The boom of Copper City manufacturing, brass,
textiles, iron castings, rubber, plastics,
Ansonia clocks, Gem nail-clippers,
toxins dumped into the lethargic Naugatuck,
waiting for 1955, and the burst
that washed the city down river, wiping
out a past, that has only begun to recover.

Someone told me that the measure of a town
is the ratio of bars and liquor stores
to churches, public buildings, and housing.
I count on Main Street, three "Christian"
churches, nestled in storefronts, two liquor
stores, ten restaurants that serve alcohol,
without adequate parking, often empty.
Old factories, reinvented, rehabilitated housing,
but at the end of the curving Main Street,
remains the husk of Farrell, and American Brass.

A town so quiet, since the exodus of all
major stores, left the mall a parking-lot.
More cars than people in the streets, passing
through to family, except on weekends,
when bars and restaurants make modest income.

Ambulance sirens blast, the armory used
for voting murmurs, not far from a Buddhist
Temple, a Catholic Church, and YMCA.
On holidays, or the Sunday fairs—life
returns, closing down blocks for revelers.

There is a mixing of neighborhood flavors, roosters
crowing in suburbia, religious gatherings blaring,
where others should not have to hear the message,
who attend their own church, respectful of others.
Speeders on motorized bikes—masked riders,
flying between parked cars, skirting
children, precipitously rude, everywhere the selfish
drive—the rush of immigration, changing faces,
language, occasional accidents, fires, disputes,
uncommon murders, unemployment, staunch conservatism.

As a younger man, I could not wait
to leave, explore the world, see things,
rip up the roots, plant new ones
but here I am—home—familial ground,
Dad's wall and sidewalk, Mom's
Barberry planted across the front yard,
a prickly reminder that yes, come down
the sidewalk, ring the bell, stay off
the grass, respect boundaries—Frost's walls,
are inherent in New England values.

Now, my beginnings have come full circle—
I feel comfortable in suburbia's predicable patterns,

where I can dig a garden, listen to children
running, screaming, knocking on doors at Halloween,
endure basketballs pounding pavement in the dark,
wake to lawnmowers, snow shovels, speak
with neighbors I've known for decades, watch
friends, confess troubles, celebrate joy,
protect each other, grow older,
suffer friends and family that pass—insomnia!

This sleepy mill town waking to reinvent
with its crisper air at the top of hills and ridges,
where even if the icecaps melt, We'll be
above sea-level to welcome new folks.

Tony Fusco

Allingtown

Independent, thickheaded, citizens of Allingtown,
we never thought of ourselves as part of West Haven.
The town trucks and police hardly ever passed our

small farm, just plenty of trailer trucks rumbling
back and forth on the Boston Post Road, targets
for snowballs and local girls sitting on the top

of billboards waving to the drivers. We had our
own center, triangle green, a hub for buses that
could take you somewhere important, New Haven

Lighthouse, Savin Rock, Bridgeport. They rolled
over routes that once were trolley and train lines
The Derby New Haven Railroad, Milford-West Shore

Yale Bowl. We waited in Fater's soda shop whose
ice cream and wax bottles of syrup made the time
 between transfers pass quickly. Right next door

Rocky's Barber Shop's a small horse on a chair
in the window lured the less than eager of the
Howdy-Doody set, and at Sal's bar, dads could

grab a fast beer. There sat the man everyone
called the mayor of Allingtown, Mr. Tamborini,
photos on the walls of former boxers Tony Carlo

Joe Harvey, Joe Pep. Where was West Haven?
We drove through it on the way to Savin Rock,
to Turk's and the stock car races, Sutcliff and Gambino
red Ford number 4 and blue Dodge number 5 waged

demolition war for 50 laps in dust and oil on Friday
nights. Santa gave out gifts in the firehouse on Admiral
Street the same room Aldo took dancing lessons

where the firemen might let you climb in a pumper truck
and ring the bell. Saturdays with a dollar each in pocket
we'd walk down US 1 past the old county home

to the Forest Theater for a matinee movie, three cartoons,
the dollar covering admission and a box of snowcaps.
Forest School waited for Monday across the street, its two
entrances, one for boys the other for girls carved in stone
lintels. We went to Lincoln up the hill, built in 1925
shortly after residents voted to separate from Orange.

Manhole covers still proclaim: Property of the town
of Orange, but they are wrong. There are signs you could
read from the bus crossing the West River: Welcome to West Haven.

But they are wrong too. Anyone that has ever lived here
knows, like we knew then, it's not on any map,
yet within these lines, lies Allingtown.

Charles Rafferty

Newtown

We brag about our corn maze, the fact our fields still accommodate some cows. It's hard to believe we're known mostly for mass murder. It's even harder to believe the shooting will one day fail to define us. On holiday weekends, the Boy Scouts set out coffee for the drunks and tired drivers. We have a dog park, occasional bears, a giant flag in the middle of the highway. The cell service is always good, and the goose shit deepens in the Ram Pasture pond. As you might have guessed, the water is both pretty and undrinkable.

Adele Evershed

Hunting

We take the scenic route to IKEA because it's fall in Connecticut, though the I-95 would be quicker, even with the traffic moving like molasses. We're on the hunt for a new sofa now that we're empty nesters. It's rained all morning, and the leaves glisten in the break of weak sunlight. We skim smoothly along roads that wiggle like worms past rivers and strip malls, past forgotten towns with houses both clapboard and clapped out. Neither of us notices their names. Then, around a bend—a *Welcome to Sandy Hook* sign—and we take a collective breath. Our boys used to play soccer here when they were in middle school, back when we'd never heard the name. Of course, now it's etched in every parent's worst nightmare.

I think back to when we first arrived in Darien. I had to take my nine-year-old daughter for her school medical. After all the prodding and temperature-taking, the pediatrician asked, "Do you have any guns in the house?" My voice came out high-pitched and crisp: "Of course not—we're British." She gave me a look—possibly pitying—and said, "You'd be surprised how many people here do." She told me to check, before every playdate, whether there were guns in the home and if they were kept in a gun safe. Did I ever do that? I can't remember.

autumn afternoon
the sudden shock
of a dead deer on the road

Brian Clements

Birds of Newtown

The more common species, of course, forage
parking lots and parks—sparrows, starlings,
robins, little black-capped chickadees—as they would
in any other place, and the Ram Pasture saturates
with the same Canada geese and the same droppings
you can find on fall stopovers in hundreds of towns.
In late spring, it is common to see turkey
crossing streets. Not in the borough,
but in neighborhoods tucked into forest,
where families prance through yards,
the little brown chicks following close behind
their mothers, the mothers behind Tom,
down into the street, dodging cars at the last second,
half trotting off to one side of the road,
half the other. Neighborhoods near Lakes Lillinonah
and Zoar are rife with raptors, red-tailed hawks
on patrol of treetops, marsh hawks invading
bogs to nest. Along Pond Brook, great blue heron
wait for trout, and yellow-bellied sapsuckers
flit among the birches. The yellow-throated vireo
has a habit of diving into windows like other
domestic dwellers: tufted titmouse,
white-breasted nuthatch, ruby-crowned kinglet, and warbler,
warbler, warbler. In the summer, marsh wren straddle
and balance on blades of marsh grass, and the edges
of woods flicker with blue jay, cardinal, eastern
bluebird, ruby throated hummingbird. A raven
competes for territory with crows. Dirt roads
abound with flycatcher, pee-wee, phoebe, kingbird,
American goldfinch flinging themselves
into flight at the slightest sign of approach,
much less the blast of a rifle's report,

which might send them into a genuine frenzy.
At night, great horned owls
terrorize the late night quiet and never migrate.
Throughout the winter, they look down from above
and stay, and stay, and stay, stubborn
like the mourning dove.

Terri Yannetti

Milford Green

Sprung up overnight
Tulips in dress uniform
Strategically poised
Around the war monuments
All standing at attention.

William Derge

Mystic, No Pizza

And indeed there was a mist.
It veiled the clapboard stores ,
and whitewashed the stone walls.
It compounded the mystery
that already paled the place.

No stopping the ten-year-olds,
who grasped the wheel of
the *Charles W. Morgon*,
and we were off for
a year or two of whales,
all of a few minutes.
It was a wonder.

How glad we were to be on equal ground
with the girls in our ignorance
of how barrels were made
from the cooper's rings and slats,
rope twisted in tracks as long as a
football field, machinery that
depended on muscle alone and
god-awful stretches of time,
the potter's world of whirl and press
the iron monger's hammer and tongs,
fire in brick, brick batter in wooden molds,
water in wood, air in sail.
It was all a wonder.

They learned so much that,
reaching the *Children's Corner*,
they felt it almost beneath them to be
tasked with constructing toy boats

from wood scraps and paper for sails.
But they were good girls,
and they didn't want to seem unkind.

We watched from the corners
Only silence from our muted phones.
It made me think of other silences.

Silenced, our sympathy for whales.
Silenced, our horror of slavery,
Silenced a memory of pestilence and plague,
the disappearance of the Pequod
and Narragansett tribes,
all that a mystique of history hides,
the past imperfect.

Mystic, Mystery, Mythical, Mistake.
All a wonder.

C.M. Rivers

Last Supper

Look, here's the deal—I'll be at Pepe's in Wooster Square,
New Haven, having two slices, one plain and one white clam,

fresh out of a 650-degree coal-fired oven, even if I have to wait
in line for an hour and change, and even if I gotta eat it

off the hood of my dead uncle's car like I did the first time
I ever had it, hands and mouth smudged with charcoal,

on a drive from Ithaca to Newport one summer, when
I stumbled across the place by accident before stepping

into an Italian bakery next door and digging
into a cannoli the size of a bulldog's head,

slot-machine cherries in my eyes, pistachios in my teeth,
and everyone singing Happy Birthday in Sicilian

to a 98-year-old woman named Lorraine, which happens
to have been my mother's name.

Jenevieve Carlyn Hughes

Sanctuary

Yale New Haven Hospital

Someone is playing *Greensleeves* on a grand piano in the atrium,
and this city hospital is everywhere & nowhere we call home.
We imagine toasting mugs of eggnog instead of coffee cups
from vending machines in the visitors' lounge, tell ourselves
there isn't anywhere we'd rather be, and for a moment
we almost believe it, in an *Auld Lang Syne* sort of way,
we're together after all, and that's what counts.

A heart on each window in the intensive care unit,
gold threading a banner at the entrance to this inner room:
an interfaith chapel becomes tabernacle, mosque, belltower,
and all the other places where love is in the waiting. We gaze
across the courtyard, where a roof garden watches over
the oncology ward: its palette, a muted patience.
This will be our world for the winter.

Steaming cartons of Vietnamese soup from outdoor carts
on Cedar Street, vendors bundled against the blistering cold,
aromatic offerings eclectic as New York's Second Avenue.
At the visitor's desk, a young woman in a *hijab* smiles,
and her presence steadies us each time we arrive;
a chorus of voices piping through the gift shop speakers,
Ethiopian hymns from *Around the World at Christmas*—
a rapt audience, we join the rows of plush-animals to listen,
buy Swiss chocolates and a child's lamb to lift our spirits,
watch the first snow of the season from a sixth-floor window,
do crossword puzzles, pace the halls, laugh at Wordle, keep vigil,

Until the announcement comes that visiting hours are ending,
so we hug our loved one as if it's the last time, just in case,

and promise to return the next day; share an elevator silence,
search for our mittens, a portal of revolving doors ushering us
into the angelic night, eyes brimming at blue lights in bare trees,
we look upward once more at the window with its heart,
step into the harkening dark.

Dolores Hayden

In the Middle Lane, Leaving New Haven

Dusk hovers behind the billboard,
We Want Your Scrap Gold,
behind the imported oil on the tank farm,
the rusting metal on the export pier,
the oversize flags on the auto dealer's lot.

Four out of five commuters drive alone.
In the left lane, a black bus
shrink-wrapped with characters for luck
hurtles past me toward the casino.
On the right, a white limo
accelerates to a wedding.

Who is the risk-taker looking for grace?

A cell tower marks frolic talk
as I exit onto narrow roads
that wind and rise and fall.
I steer into the shapes of time:

River Street and Water Street
curve toward fishermen's work,
Leete's Island Road weaves
where farmers grew salt hay
and the last of the light fades
on bone-colored spartina.

Who is the survivor mapping local history?

On Colonial Road, a developer
has been clearing to build.
Dispossessed, a doe and a buck
wander onto the asphalt—
pay attention!

Braking hard, headlights high,
I hear an owl.
I might as well be an owl,
hooting at the ice,
lecturing the winter.

Snow coats the sand on the beach, snow drifts
over the sea wall next to the Sound.
On Cove Lane, my house resists
the January wind, windows dark.

My house is as cold as only a widow's can be.
On the porch: shovel, rock salt, firewood.

Ruth Hoberman

In Abeyance

New Haven clings
to a ragged beauty—

train whistles, gulls,
and sirens,

the disheveled lost drifting
into intersections

under the billboards' offer:
Hit by a car? Call me!

Sunlit buildings shoulder
the street, red bricks

radiant. I can almost
forgive myself

on this day when nothing
has gone wrong

and even the courthouse,
pale and pillared,

manages a certain stiff grace.
Sometimes

what chases us rests—hounds,
winter, remorse—held,

like the brass-players' horns,
still

in somebody's lap
for a measure.

Ruth Hoberman

With my Granddaughter at the Peabody Museum

The squid's gigantic, eyes like black globes,
tentacles outstretched over the vestibule.
It gives me pause, taking a toddler in.

Look! I say and she does, at huge gray skeletons
posed on iron posts: no flesh, all color gone,
as if dinosaurs lived in a clatter of bones.

Time cascades through the cavernous halls.
She runs ahead, thrilled to move alone
past a seven-foot bear stepping from rocky scrub,

past bobcats and bison, as the river piles the rest of us—
dinosaurs, squid, mammals, birds, the grandparents bent
over strollers—into the bracken along its banks,

thrusting her toward—toward what? What future
have we gifted you with, oh my granddaughter,
my daughter, my bones?

The Way It Was

Fred Gerhard

My Father Teaches Me to Drive the Trolley

My father and I are now motormen
at the Shoreline Trolley Museum in East Haven, Connecticut

My father came back to me in my lost years,
took one look at my eyes so full they spoke
and asked, "Would you like to run the trolleys with me?"

Would I like to drive the trolleys?!
And join him dressed in black
jacket, hat, vest with the pocket-watch chain
slung silver through a buttonhole?

And so, he teaches me again to move the ancient streetcar,
all of it. Watching his hands, my hands,
push the key forward with a click,
toggle the brake handle aside to let off pressure
with a long whoosh,
stomp the metal disk on the floor to the bell below
twice to go,
and pull the large controller knob
hesitating through each notch,
motors rising pitch at each pop
drawing power, dimming lights,
picking up speed on gleaming rails.
"Just let it coast awhile."
Listen
for the clicks and clacks
and the pole above the wooden roof jostling like a drum
through the junction
above a switch
thrown
for the next journey.

Havi Brouillard

Rails to Trails, Vernon, Connecticut

There is a ghost train that lives down the street from my childhood
    house.
Its horn echoes far, eerie and pulsing into the dawn and dusk.
Centuries ago, its line brushed against my neighborhood,
carting supplies to Manchester or Ellington.
The power poles are rotting now,
the old pump shed torn down to make way for raised ranches.
A plaque commemorates its previous existence.
The old turntable is nothing but a circular pit of stone and gravel.

But the horn still remains.
It echoes through the valley of my home, resolute,
even if the train has been scrapped for parts.
It lingers in the way young children beg their parents
to honk their mini van's horn in the old keystone tunnel.
It shines through morning sun and vivid cloud sunsets,
and it loves to scare the shit out of me.

As I walk the gravel of the old rail line, I can feel
the rumbling of the old tracks embedded deep within the earth.
There's not much left, and what's there is frozen in time,
encased in history by signs and placards.
The metal was salvaged years ago, reclaimed for something greater.
But if you listen closely, past the bluejays and the crows,
you might still hear the train.

Julia M. Paul

Homework Assignment

Manchester

The boy's eyes dart around a room
thick with knick-knacks: ceramic poodles,
flowerless vases, harlequin clown figurines
arranged on dust-free shelves. Portraits
of whiskered men and laced-up women
stare down from walls papered
in a faded cabbage rose pattern.

He twitches in the horse-hair stuffed chair.
The woman time has shrunken
to his size sits opposite. The boy
is here for an assignment—
interview someone in your town.

A town is shaped by its ghosts,
Thelma Woodbridge begins.
The darting eyes open wide, then settle.
Ghosts?

Oh yes, ghosts! All around us,
the spirits of those who walked this ground,
worked this soil, whose bones are buried here.
Deep in this soil: arrowheads, broken bits
of carved and shaped stone—
tools of the Podunks.
Deep in this soil, shards of glass
from the Pitkin Glass Factory—
imperfect and grainy as memory.
Deep in this soil, the sweat of farmers,
tobacco pickers, factory workers, smithies and soldiers.

In the air we breathe in this house,
the ghost of Electa Woodbridge,
who fetched a cup of water
for George Washington when he stopped
at her daddy's tavern, over there,
where the Shell station is now.

Electa went on to marry George Cheney;
their eight sons revolutionized the silk industry.
Their spirits are everywhere—
in the schools they built, the mills,
houses for workers, the mansions on the hill.
These buildings hold their stories.

Miss Mary, the daughter of the youngest
brother—you can almost still see her
riding down Main Street in her ancient car,
her driver deaf to the honking.
If you listen with your eyes closed,
you can hear the children in Miss Mary's
garden—how they laugh and clap
and clamor for another story! Can you
see Miss Mary seated before them
with a picture book on her lap?

Her spirit is in the children and their
children's children. When Miss Mary's
paperboy was hit by a car, she paid
for his care, gave him, a poor immigrant,
money for college. He became a doctor.
Her spirit lived in him and in the lives he touched.
So you see, young man,
this town is shaped by its ghosts,

Dig deep in this soil.
Close your eyes to better see the sachems,
settlers, selectmen, silk workers.
Like the crooked tree in my yard
with its hungry roots, feast on the rich layers
of the past. Let the ghosts gather in you.
Listen well to their stories.

Garrett Phelan

The Chrome Plating Line at Pratt & Whitney

We hooked up large jet engine parts,
raised them with the push of a button,
moved them over huge vats
and then lowered them into the chemicals.

He was 64 years old, a year away from retirement
after 45 years on the chrome plating line.
When he was told to work with the college kid,
I could feel he wanted to work alone.

One day we were told to stop and move back from the line.
The cyanide man had arrived.
He wore rubber boots, a rubber apron and huge rubber gloves
and dropped new cyanide eggs into the first vat.

After a few weeks my clothes began disintegrating.
Little splashes ate away my t-shirt, dungarees,
even my Converse All Stars started to disappear.

You couldn't take a shit in private.
Above the factory floor were 6 toilet stalls with no doors
so the foreman could catch you slacking.
Reading with *The Hartford Courant*
was the only way to cover yourself.

He could disappear in the middle of a word—
you never caught him in the bathroom.
He could smell a foreman before I could see one.
He taught me how to disappear—like grease sucked out
of an engine part lowered into the degreaser.

He taught me how to work when there was no work,
He taught me how the chrome plating line could
eat away more than your clothes,
He taught me if you keep disappearing enough,
no one would know your name.

John Long

Industrial Heartland

What sins
made this city
paradise lost?
Our old life
with factory jobs
   legendary,
a clean river with trout
   beautiful
in fading memory.

When this city
grew brick factories
along the riverbank,
companies needed us.
We made it home.
   Optimism
never questioned
   prosperity
guaranteed for all.

A single brick,
falling loose, can
collapse a building.
One company, leaving,
starts an avalanche.
   Fearfulness,
we saw it grow.
   Uncertainty
tore us apart.

Who answers
for lives
chewed up, spit out?
Companies pull out
for greener pastures.
     Progress
leaves us behind,
     expendable—
belly up like dead fish.

Pat Mottola

Cheshire Jewels

"Everyone in Cheshire, at some time or other, works in the Button Shop."
—Edward Gumprecht, The One Hundred Years of Button
Manufacturing in Cheshire

In the quiet brick building by the river
where dust lies thick as stories,
workers' voices are awakened by the sound
of poetry and music, artists in the courtyard—
the Ball & Socket Factory alive again.

They speak of how button production
in Cheshire was part of Connecticut's
pioneering role in the precision manufacturing
revolution of the nineteenth century,
a kingdom built with small round things,
buttons of brass, vegetable ivory, and glass.

Anna worked there for 50 years,
since 1928. She fed parts into a foot press,
using foot power to stamp out the buttons—
her foot impression ingrained in her foot pedal,
given to her when she retired.

Edward worked in the factory for 62 years—
started in 1886 at the age of 15. One of his daily
assignments: to see that all the lamps were filled
with kerosene and hung from each machine.
Working ten hours a day six days a week.

Small children speak up too—
employed because they could be paid less
than adults. In 1880 the youngest, William,
was ten. His small body would fit under

dangerous machinery to retrieve parts.
There he learned to count—the brass buttons,
uniform buttons for Union and Confederate forces,
and for American troops during two world wars.

But most famous, the coveted *Cheshire Jewels*,
fancy buttons made from brass-backed glass,
desirable for their beauty, these shimmering gems.
In the Victorian Era, ladies gathered these buttons
on a string—a *charm string*, a *love string*—
a sentimental keepsake of their admirers.

Today, the factory echoes with the sound of
footsteps just like those that graced the buildings
for 150 years, their history embedded for all time
like the buttons that fell, small secrets pressed
into the floor, set like quiet stars.

Vivian Shipley

Frances Splettstocher, 21

February 1925, first dial painter to die in Waterbury; I had
lip-pointed for 4 years, did think it strange that my handkerchief
glowed in the dark when I blew my nose, but church members,
makers of Waterbury's Dollar Watches, wouldn't let young girls
like us do anything harmful. First I mixed glue, water, radium
powder to make glowing greenish-white paint, then applied it
with a camel hair brush to dial numbers. A few strokes, brushes
lost their shape and I couldn't paint accurately. My teacher told
me to point the brush with my lips. I did this about six times for
every watch dial. The paint didn't taste funny—it didn't have
taste. Next to me racks of altimeters and clock dials waited

like upturned faces of children I would never have. I was
proud of Marie Curie who won two Nobel Prizes for discovering
liquid sunshine. How could I know it would be my embalming
fluid or that in 1922, Amelia Maggia died in Orange, NJ,
jawbone so rotten that the dentist lifted her entire mandible out
of her mouth. US Radium recorded cause of death as *syphilis,*
didn't mention chemists used lead screens, masks and tongs
to handle radium while Amelia sucked in death. My friend Elsie
told me not to have a tooth pulled but in February, 1925, I did.
The hole in my cheek would not heal; my uncle would pay
me a dime to go away so he did not have to look at it.

At least I wasn't like Katherine Moore who slapped radium
around like it was cake frosting. With a grapefruit size tumor
jutting from her chin, her jaw was so deformed she didn't go
out in public without pulling her coat collar up. My family
worked in the clock factory, my father had *spelter shakes,*
my uncle *metal fume fever,* my brother *brass founder's ague.*
Quailing, my father was sure radium poisoning was killing me;
he dared not make any kick about it because he'd lose his job.

My own words dogpaddled, even when I listened to my heart,
cold disc of stethoscope on my chest, blood punching chambers
like fists in kid gloves nice girls like me wore in the 1920s.

José B. González

Along Mystic's Pequot Avenue

Along the wall along the shore
along the colonials along the sand,
they planted signs that said
no   trespassing.

Across the sweetgum along
the fence along the harbor,
they posted a sign that warns,
no   fishing.

Along the middle of the town,
they set poles along the edges
of concrete, they posted
street signs that read
Pequot Avenue.

Along, along, along,
they set a sign
of the massacre,
the memory of the blaze,
the scalping, the burns, set
a far distance from crowds.

Vivian Shipley

May 25, 1647, Gov. John Winthrop Recorded the First Execution for Witchcraft in the New World: [   ] of Windsor, Connecticut

Your death, your town of Windsor were noted
but not your name. [   ], you were hung
in Hartford for having *consulteth with a familiar*

spirit and developing a relationship with Satan.
Stripped of your name, your clothing, dread
must have pulsed within you. Searched for signs

of the devil, there was no teat in a secret place
where the Devil could suck, or blue and red spots
like a flea biting or flesh sunken into a hollow.

Finding nothing, judges were persuaded you had
covered them but in time they would come again.
[   ], sitting through sermons peppered with

Hell's abyss, you had always feared for your future.
Long days came to a close, putting your face against
muslin of your pillow, did you imagine being put

on trial, accused as no one had ever been? Did you
feel breathing grow difficult, your spirit slowly
compressing? [   ], you knew there were

no witches—but with red hot irons, scalding water,
you were certain you'd be compelled to believe.
A name passed doorstep to doorstep was [   ]

when goats were lost to wolves, crops to floods
along the Connecticut River. 1647, influenza and
smallpox, dozens of deaths were laid at your feet.

[   ], why didn't your husband protest?
Owner of land in Windsor, could it be he believed
there was no way to predict who would become

a witch, was reminded that you would not cleave
through thicket and vine to forage for medicinal
teas with the other women. The gallows were near

Hartford's Old State House; everyone could see.
After you were cut down and carted away, [   ],
to hold in their fear, women closed ranks, walked

close together, tried to outdo one another, quoting
verses from the Bible: *Thou shalt not suffer a witch
to live. Exodus (22:18)* Even when your daughter,

Alice Young Beamon, was accused of witchcraft
30 years later in Springfield MA, you were not
named. For almost 250 years, you were [   ].

By 1891, discovery of the diary of Matthew Grant,
Windsor Town Clerk, unearthed an entry dated
May 25, 1647, that filled in the blank: [Alyse Young].

Megan Leonard

A Haunting

This one is a ghost story and this time the ghost is a witch. The witch named Mercy was beautiful, they say, beautiful past her years. If a woman is too beautiful or too ugly that woman is a witch. In this ghost story, Mercy is beautiful and she also has a temper. You know about that—your mother had a temper. Your mother's mother had a temper. That mother use to shake a fry pan at you if her temper got too bad—it was all they remembered of her after she died, because the only thing that matters about a mother is how good-tempered and sweet she is.

This witch Mercy has a mean tone of voice when she gets mad, and she tells her neighbor to skit—her neighbors decide to kill her for this. Mercy's tone of voice   Mercy's anger and her neighbors' decision is carefully preserved in the court documents. It's important for a woman to not be too beautiful and definitely not be too ugly, and it's important for that woman to always smile. When her neighbors cheat her over the price of a pig, she should smile. When her neighbors call her a witch and spit on her, she should smile. When her neighbors tell her they will kill her, she should smile, and she should definitely not say she would rip them to pieces if she could. She could not, after all, rip them to pieces: she is a woman, and she is much smaller in size and fewer in number than the neighbors. Mercy says this to the judge, who writes it down and saves it. Mercy forgot to smile enough, and Mercy got angry too many times, and now they know she is a witch.

In this ghost story, Mercy begs to be thrown in the pond, knowing she can't swim. In this ghost story, they don't even let her change her pond-soaked wool dress before they shackle her in the jail cell. In this ghost story, she doesn't die to become a ghost. Instead, she lives: she returns to her home in her rat-chewed dress, months later, after months of darkness in the cell, and she doesn't say a word to her neighbors ever again and she always does smile, she never forgets to smile again. Because now she is a ghost, instead of a witch.

D. Walsh Gilbert

The Rock at the Todd-Wadsworth Smallpox Inoculation Hospital, 1790s Farmington

Grizzle-gray bedrock bared from the hardwood forest
of Rattlesnake Mountain. Old as the stars.
Near the stony goat pasture on old Settlement Road
and far from the center of town.
A flat traprock ledge set in the sunshine.
If you look, and look closely, you can find it.

After inoculation with a smidgeon of live pus—
the spit of the devil of smallpox—quarantined patients
isolated for weeks at the wood-made Hospital, 1790s.
Today, only cellar hole, a mortarless foundation.
But the rock nearby still lives. Hospital Rock.
Where families left parcels for the ones they loved.

And the people lived. Engraved their names forever—
R.S. Norton, Caleb Bacon, Mary Pitkin—carved
signatures of those who were scratched with traces
of something invisible. Pinpricked with a beast
they feared but faced. Brave enough to trust and try.
To survive. And the outcrop never winced

although Hospital Rock was as inscribed as its people.
A tombstone marking the death of a pestilence
John Adams called the king of terrors.
A vital, living monument. The rock still waits and listens.
It's kissed every quiet daybreak since.
Weed-hidden. Time-hardened. Alive in Farmington.
Bold, and daring to remember.

Steve R. Veilleux

Twilight on Thompson Hill

It's twilight on Thompson Hill and I with Lil
on a long leash am still with my thoughts
and hers on the Common,
an early Autumn breeze swirling leaves and memories.

It's twilight on Thompson Hill
a lone Ford pickup approaches the Stop Sign,
a lone driver heading home
anticipating a quiet evening,
hope of a filling meal, a place to lay his shoes.

Lil tilts her head on Thompson Hill
a seeming interest in the orange turning
dusk through the windows of the Mason House,
painted now with the warmth of the setting sun,
and soon the dimming violets of twilight.

The electric lights of the grand old homes on Thompson Hill
mark the evening;
the half-lights of Fairie fill the dusk
and Lil sniffs at the cooling air upon the Green
and stops when she spies the first crossing
of the Spirits on Thompson Hill.

First upon the Green, outfitted in his finest Victorian clothes,
larger than life, as he was when at his tavern's doors he stood,
Vernon Stiles, and by his side and equally wide
his stately wife, Lucy Goddard.
In the half-light, Lil pauses to sniff
at a growing thickness in the air.

A car horn flares, then fades in the distance
replaced by the clop clop of horse hooves,
the crunching of loose stone and wet earth beneath carriage wheels,
the glimmer of candlelight from the shops along the way,
an open window, a long-skirted woman over the hearth,
a warm loaf in hand.

And we become aware of the faces from a past age,
the vital Barons, Savin and Wilkinson, Grosvenor and Mason, Nichols
            and Watson.
Even now, they tower over the others,
though their heads are bowed,
as if some understanding has pierced this realm,
an entanglement of spirit passing through one another as they could
            never in life

And the voices cry as one on Thompson Hill—
those who tilled the soil, those who milled the grain,
who tamed the rivers, tamed the rain,
who grew the land, who brewed the ale,
who watch over these homes from beyond the pale.

For every mill and every mansion, for every man with vision,
here stand those who opened the canals to power the mills,
to clothe and feed the Hills of Thompson,
who dug up the bones of the earth, and built the walls,
who shaped the bricks and mortared the stone,
and left their souls upon Thompson Hill.

The press of souls with picks and hoes, with workman's awls and axes,
these are the men and girls, the women and boys
whose brows were wet with sweat and mortar,
whose spirit remains on Thompson Hill,

Our driver now, he looks both ways,
releases the clutch and crosses the road by Thompson Hill,
and I with Lil, a casual wave
and we both towards home for another day.

Chris Abbate

Hartford Circus Fire

July 6, 1944

The Flying Wallendas,
highwire act without a net,
beneath the big top—
waterproofed
with paraffin wax
and gasoline
in case of rain.

Then, a flicked cigarette,
or an arsonist.
Still, no one knows.
The band plays
"The Stars and Stripes Forever"—
the Disaster March,
a distress signal to carnies.

Only eight minutes
before consummation,
enough time for a young boy
to dash from his front row seat,
tethered to his father's hand
ahead of a stampede
of people and animals.

This link in the chain
of fathers and sons.
How each carried
the seed of another
away from the burning tent
that hot, summer day.

Without his father,
no young boy.
And without the young boy,
no me.

Sandra Yannone

The Ten Worst Fires in U.S. History

Imagine waking to a long-anticipated summer
deluge, early morning before no one else is awake,

just you and a symphony of water
making its music known. Now imagine

it is the next day, only eighty years earlier,
the morning thick with humidity and the sun

rising, a throbbing like a toothache in the upper
jaw, the grounds below not anticipating

the afternoon's scars of scorched earth, charred
bones, human flesh sloughing off

circus dwellers like candle wax. Now imagine
as you listen to the rain's welcome

relief that there is an eight-year-old boy
waking to an entire day of what comes next

except today reigns extraordinary. Today
the circus is in town, just down the street

from the boy's house doused in his father's alcohol,
but he, the boy, doesn't really understand

the difference between flammable and combustible,
between alcohol and kerosene, between paraffin

and candle wax, although both will coat the boy's childhood
with an ominous smell. At eight, the boy is prone to bicycles

and boomerangs, rare coins and postage stamps, common
scrapes and burns. Now imagine you imagining all this

because this long-ago boy is your not-so-long-gone father
who asks a nine-year-old you if you've read anything

about a circus fire as you sit reading yet another
book about disasters—this one about the ten worst

fires in U.S. history—and when you look up
from the pages, wide-eyed, drunk

with wonder, and blow a drawn out "Yeah"
like an exaggerated kiss, he returns the volley

with a flat "I was there" and walks away.
It will be well over another decade

before you hear anything about the fire again
and even decades more before he shares

the full story unprompted like penny candy,
almost as if he loves the story coated in wax,

ready to go up in smoke. For years, you know
you will write this story, but you don't know

what the story is. You don't know the boy
or the girl eager to climb down each dangling

rope from the ends of the high wire. Now
the boy is dead two years. Now tomorrow,

the 80th anniversary of the circus fire looms
like burnt smoke over water. Now you are

both the boy and the girl and the only one
left to tell this story. Now the rain

has stopped its astonishing percussion. Now
what remains: a clattering of invisible bird songs.

The sun beginning its unabashed rise to burn.

Ginny Lowe Connors

The Mark Twain House

Piloting a steamboat along the Mississippi—
ah, those were the days. Pull up a chair and he'll tell
you one story after another of his life on the river.
He's settled down now. More or less.

So then this house. To hold the stories, hold his family close,
hold him up as a man of means. Man of accomplishment.
His house stately as a steamboat, plowing through Hartford's
rumpled air. Red brick and splash. Gaudy and gabled.

A restless traveler, Sam adores the exotic.
His home's entryway is a Turkish bazaar. Plush carpets,
oriental vases, exotic stencils, rich carvings.
A barefoot boy travelled a long way. He said, *I have arrived.*

The family's cats become lions and tigers stalking
and pouncing in the conservatory—a jungle of green.
Sunlight dazzles the rubber plants. Is it fountain or waterfall
that burbles and cascades? Every day the place must be tamed again.

Sometimes Sam himself is the jungle cat, and little Jean rides him
into the library. This room's another story that three little girls demand.
A whisper, sudden exclamation, a mystery, a warning.
Start with the cat in a ruff and include all items on the mantle.

Within this boisterous household, the master bedroom
is a benediction. Cherubs emerge from a bed
elaborate with carvings. Pillows go at the foot of the bed
so Sam and Livy's drowsy eyes can gaze upon angels before sleep.

Cigar smoke and whiskey mark the billiard room.
Friday nights, friends gather, knock balls across green felt,
tell tall tales, turn the air blue. Most days, Sam hunches
over the corner desk. Scribbling, reflecting, crossing out.

Tom, Huck and Jim live here, and a prince, a pauper.
Ghosts of them still roam the Twain house,
though the family is gone. A Connecticut Yankee
peers out the window, betting on an eclipse.

The rags of love remain. Walls listen as Sam swears
at a new-fangled gadget, the telephone. Livy
clucks her tongue. Baby Langdon reaches out
his chubby arms. That moaning may be the wind.

It may be Susy, delirious with meningitis. Brilliant girl
full of fire, full of plans. How alone she is at the end.
Fortune and catastrophe, sorrow and celebration
find each other here. As in any great story.

Elizabeth Alexander

Allegiance

Teacher is bewildered when packages
and letters come from far to say how brave,
how visionary, how stare-down-the-beast
is Prudence Crandall of Canterbury.
Work, she says, there is always work to do,
not in the name of self but in the name,
the water-clarity of what is right.
We crave radiance in this austere world,
light in the spiritual darkness.
Learning is the one perfect religion,
its path correct, narrow, certain, straight.
At its end it blossoms and billows
into vari-colored polyphony:

the sweet infinity of true knowledge.

Gwen North Reiss

Louis Kahn

Yale Center for British Art, New Haven

His structures channel light, lend shadows stone,
concrete, and steel. The door recedes, the stair
is not an announcement. You're on your own.
Inside, the bordered light of a city square.

Sheltered and outsized spaces open
each to another like a ship steered into port
or moored to the pump and spin of a silent drum
or the height of center atrium and court.

Geometry links into chambered simplicity,
a composition half-tamed into rooms.
Of architecture, he said, "There is a speaking
which is not speech." The seasons enter

as light seeks a formal frame and bathes the eye
and a roof is understudy to the sky.

Maxine Susman

Florence Griswold's Boardinghouse

"Birthplace of American Impressionism," Lyme, Connecticut

A grand old house, her childhood home
but how rattle around in it alone,
her family gone, no money to keep it?

She loved the views from upstairs windows,
the back lawn giving on the lush-banked river
that rose and fell in changing tides of color,
fields nearby, cattle munching on salt hay—

one by one they came by rail up from the City
and rented rooms, having heard how the light lifted,
tidal shifts played shapes on the horizon,

Hassam, Metcalf, others, one summer to the next
would drink their breakfast coffee on her porch
then pile into the wagon and set off for the dunes.

The French were painting *en plein air*, why not here?
The new folding easels, pigments in metal tubes—
artists could work in all varieties of light
and paint not exactly what they saw.

Their ideas, egos, breakthroughs, parlor games—
Florence presided, artful choreographer
providing space for fresher prospects, novel scenes
away from their boilerplate city studios,

she kept her garden drenched in flowers,
served good food and heady conversation,
hung their paintings up for sale in the front hall.

Katharyn Howd Machan

Roxbury, 1956

I saw her, once, when I was
so small the unpaved Connecticut road
seemed a highway of shimmering
suns. My grandmother's voice

introduced me to Hazel, old
woman who lived there without
running water, who peered at me
hard, said *Her eyes will go green.*

Summer was just coming in,
I'm sure, air warm enough
for windows to be wide, and I
listened in my speechless shyness

where weeds tickled my grandmother's
tires, the skirt of my new-to-me
checked cotton thin dress.
She hauls the bucket for me

sometimes, and buys me groceries
I need—my ears catching
Hazel's words, my grandmother's nodding
murmur, surprise. And then the smooth

wheels on pebbles and sand, sleek
convertible, brilliant white top down:
blond hair in a silken scarf,
dark glasses, horn's honk, fingers' wave—

*There she is now! Going home to Mr.
Miller.* Hazel's voice, simply accepting,
and me wondering why my grandmother
whispered *Marilyn*, stars in her eyes.

Bill Conlon

The Lady Wore Cleats

Twenty years old in 1961,
she struck out Ted Williams
in an exhibition. That's right—she.
Joan Joyce threw a softball, hard and fast.
Teddy Ballgame named this girl
the toughest pitcher he had ever faced.
Most never heard of the woman,
one of the greatest American athletes.

Joan played softball on the national
and international levels for two decades,
pitching 150 no-hitters, striking out 10,000 batters,
while hitting .327 lifetime. She mesmerized
hitters and enchanted this wide-eyed boy.
She spent winters as an all-American A.A.U.
basketball player, scoring 67 points in one game,
30 per game before the three-point shot.

A month after learning to bowl,
Joan won the Connecticut state title.
Later, Joan made the LPGA Tour, scored
a tournament record round of 17 putts at age 42.
How's them apples, Tiger? I watched the woman,
inducted into 19 halls of fame, play a prelim
basketball game in Ansonia. Bill Spivey,
seven feet when seven feet meant tall,
drew the crowd. Joan stole the show.

    Joan Joyce coached young women at F.A.U.
    for 28 years until she died in March of '22 at 81.

On your toes up there, fellas.
Here she comes—hard and fast.

Steve Straight

Old Longtooth

—for the Hill-Stead Museum, Farmington, Connecticut

During a drought in 1913 the Italian workmen,
struggling to dig a water trench on the grounds
of the great estate, kept stubbing their shovels
on thick roots of something well below
the waterlogged turf, until one of them
stopped and called out, "Non radice, ossa, ossa!"

And sure enough, as they felt their way
with their fingers now, down through the sticky clay,
they did find bones, heavy and ancient,
what the professor called in from Yale
would confirm was *Mammut americanum*,
the American mastodon.

It's not hard to imagine this stocky elephant of old
standing in the late Pleistocene winter,
his shaggy brown coat dusted with snow
as the flexible trunk grabs twigs and
branches from the lark, spruce, and pine
in the Hill-Stead hills fifteen thousand years ago
as the glaciers retreat to the north.

There are no buildings, of course, no buildings at all,
and the very occasional neighbors are the dire wolf,
the short-faced bear, a beaver of three hundred pounds,
or the giant ground sloth lumbering by in the forest.

Nine feet at the shoulder, with curved tusks just as long,
he was a solitary being, browsing his fill
a full-time job at a weight of five tons,

cracking off limbs with his tusks and
grinding them down with his nipple-shaped molars.

At death there was "no sign of foul play,"
as the professor said, no proof of Clovis hunters
taking him down, just a few thousand years
from extinction, anyway, having roamed the earth
for a million. Tuberculosis may have claimed him.

If one were still around, as Jefferson had hoped,
no doubt it would be chained somewhere, trotted out
for show under threat of the bullhook, a spectacle
in a world that seems to feed on celebrity.

Whatever drew you to this swampy depression,
moss or pinecones or just a drink of pure water,
I for one am glad you are not here today
to see this circus, this three-ring earth.

Sarah P. Blanchard

Woodstock in stones

I
Those early settlers understood
nothing of glaciers but knew
how to work with
what the icepack abandoned:
granite, slate, feldspar, shale—
stones hoisted into walls and cellars
fitted curve to notch
for chapels and shelters.

Creators of churches must also build barns
to house both sinners and innocents
to shelter newborn calves, autumn harvests,
the bounty of labor: grapes, grains, virtues.
Here is blood with body
manure, meat, redemption.
Everything shouldered
stone on stone on stone.

II
Every story arcs toward an ending.
Stones proclaim endings as they hold
stories beneath skins of moss and lichen.
Each rough-cut name, a long story
dimpling the granite on Woodstock Hill:
Bowen, Hammond, Perrin, Child, Peake.

But there are far older stories.
Look away from the Hill. Go instead
to the valleys and deep hollows
where bedrock holds other memories—
a closer knowledge of ice and earth:

the rude bounty abandoned by glaciers
then found, shaped by more ancient hands:
flaked flint and quartz, cairns and bannerstones.
Find *those* names, whispered only on faint winds
Pequot, Nipmuc, Mohegan, Wabbaquasset.

III
All stoneworkers lose fingerprints.
Muscle and sinew grow with work
but ridges and whorls disappear.
Rock smooths flesh into a
flatness of callus and corn
adding anonymous layers of
skin, leather, mold, lichen—
until who we are
becomes defined only by
what we heft from the earth
and why.

Brad Davis

Among Erratics

I am drawn to the changeless,
to what appears to be exactly the same
yesterday, today, forever,
like the erratics punctuating
our local state park's time-sculpted terrain.

So let us consider erratics, original
settlers set down, dispersed by retreating
ice as modest testimony
to a frozen age
inconceivable to me now—the ice a mile thick

above our West Putnam condo and around
these parts for ten thousand years.
I am drawn to erratics,
their silence, their wordless word
of mastodons and Paleoindians, those of our kind

who, for another ten thousand years,
camped among these massive, telltale stones—as
among grandfathers and grandmothers—
before strangers arrived
in boats and assumed priority,

their new governing
as glacial as that old smothering ice
and subtle as a virus.
Will we, their offspring, ever learn
and recede to permit the land its renewal?

Till then, I'm done with language,
pretty as a flower or marbled with irony—
drawn now to plainness
as erratics are plain
and forthright and wholly without shame.

In All Weathers

Gretchen Fletcher

After Frost

> *... the wise trees*
> *stand sleeping in the cold ...*
> *The half-stripped trees*
> *struck by a wind together ...*
> —*Robert Frost*

Winter woods in Connecticut look
like a clatter of woven baskets
beating each other
to the punch, shattering
      silent spaces
between trees with a confounded
impassable tangle of dry, hacking coughs,
smacking sticks entwined this way and that,
a branched cacophony that tapers
      to a whisper
of clicking twigs, all held aloft
by thick-barked trunks
      standing silent
beside stone walls, bravely
holding up their end of the bargain:
to bear the brunt of winds and ice
that coat and snap those of lesser mettle
than these old New Englanders.

Anne Hampford

First Snow

It's still snowing
among the pines
down by the reservoir.
Or so it seems
on this crisp morning,
when a breeze
looses powder
from the branches,
blurring the forest.

Another waft
and I am flurried—
tiny crystals
tingle my face
shimmer in the early light.

The woodland settles.
Snow-laden limbs
bend earthward.
Drifts slow my progress
as I ascend the ridge
to where the trees thin
and the path opens.
Wren-song greets me.
I inhale the resinous air,
bow to the abrupt red
of a lone winterberry.

Cortney Davis

This Is a Poem about Snow

The snow falling on Ferris Avenue
filling the apartment parking lot
the winter after the divorce
when my kids were five and three
our first-floor apartment looking out
at cars and the stairs that led to the basement
the year I worked in the operating room
7-3 shift, always tired, always scrimping
and now snow was piling up, sparkling
in the just-coming-on fluorescent lights
snow so pure, not yet dirty with ash
from garbage burning somewhere
in Norwalk and the kids were begging
to go outside, to go outside
but it was cold, and I kept saying
tomorrow or *after dinner*
until they were almost crying with desire
so I bundled them in their puffy suits
hats and scarves and mittens on strings
boots with buckles then, not Velcro
and let them go out alone
through the cement hall, out the clanging door
watching from the kitchen window
as they tipped up their faces to see how snow
flashed and glittered against the dark sky
threw snow into the air and at each other
ran to catch the sparkles, their snow shadows
growing longer or shorter as they played
looking to see if I was truly watching
until snow crept under their collars
fingers grew numb and a certain loneliness
called them back inside where I lifted them

from their wet clothes and felt their icy
cheeks against mine, praised the snowman
they'd tried to make for me, then turned away
remembering how I'd said *I'll wait here*
when it should have been me
teaching them the swish of arm and leg
to make perfect snow angels
the trick of packing feathery snow
and how the world twirled and grew dizzy
as I held them whirling, safe, present
in the magic of this particular snow
that would be gone by morning

Sue Ellen Thompson

Connecticut in March

Here where everything is granite—
from the steps that prop the baby
for her first spring photograph
to the stones gossiping in the cemetery
two doors down—even the green
is lined with gray, and from
the blood-red buds just breaking
will come leaves of waxy green
that raise their hands as if in protest,
showing palms of silver.

I have been to California, I have seen
the coastal evergreens, their skirts reversed,
blown seaward. I have watched the ocean
darken and fold, as if drawing out a secret
from the land. I have stood among the succulents,
sun on my back like a shawl of fire,
thinking of wet bark, leaf rot, grass as pale and matted
to the frozen ground as to a brow in fever.

I have tried to love a place
for the helpless goodness of its weather,
for the light that spends itself on everything,
confident of being overlooked.
I've traveled north to where
the sun stands watch like a man without trust,
listening all night while his young wife sleeps,
and I have walked Caribbean beaches
where the various blues amalgamate
to a lover's breath, less air than ardor.

But I am married to this late winter bog,
this grayscape, this
aluminum sky that when it rains
reveals the best and worst that can be said
of any marriage: that it endured.

John Muro

Overwintering

I'm undone by days such as this, with sunlight
just arriving, the color of mead, washing across
the undulating drifts that run along the fence-
line like main-sails placed one after the other
while elsewhere the snow's spattered against
furrows of tree bark as if it is seeking a way
to clamber back to heaven, or at least to the
understory where a few hush-winged birds
still sleep, sharing their perch with a sky of
improbable blue and a queue of listless clouds
and, yet, despite the stillness and the cold,
I find myself grateful for air that's clove-scented
and a land that's littered with felled branches,
upturned stones and shells of ice glistening
like fractured pieces of antique glass, free of
sound and motion, and still months from the
thaw and frenetic rush towards rebirth and
the gradual unveiling of an overturned earth.

Sara Shea

From the Mire

I was eight, barely old enough to know
more than the shape of my own wonder—
skipping home from second grade
in galoshes, parka zipped to my chin.

I ducked beneath gnarled laurels,
crawled the narrow, secret path
past the swamp—black vernal pools
whispering between the school grounds
and the wide, quiet lawns
of our Connecticut street.

It was March, a time when trees stood bare
when crusts of snow clung to shadowed gullies,
and the world felt half-dreamed and half-awake.

I lingered at the edge—took a hesitant step
toward dark water, where wonder
still lay submerged, a half-remembered song.

In summertime, magic had reigned here
when dragonflies danced like living jewels
and pollywogs surged. I'd unearthed snails,
newts, traced raccoon tracks, glimpsed herons.

Now the swamp lay hushed.
I tested icy fringes. Slick black muck
crept past the cuff of my boot.
Then from the mire an unbidden shimmer:
a dark spire, purple as a bruise,
tender and obscene as a tongue.

Something luminous rising
against winter's dull palette.
A beast's horn? A hawk's hooked beak?
Silken slipper of a sleeping elf?
Its mystery was enough.

I pried that smooth, feral treasure
from the swamp's cold clutch,
gagging at its fetid breath—
garlic, earth, death, and birth
and carried it home to my father
who turned it in his hands, then smiled
at this secret only seasons could know—

Ah, springtime! The skunk cabbage spathe.

Ralph Earle

New National Historic Park

Impressionists from New York City used to summer at the Weir Farm, a mile up the road from our home, and after our time it became a National Historic Park, whose white clapboards and lichen-crusted granite speak of the small quiet world I was born into.

In the April drizzle, I follow the path between stone walls, where John Singer Sargent and Childe Hassam once strolled through a meadow. Now a forest has sprung up, and around the pond where they swam and painted, a new green carpet of skunk cabbage.

I walk in the shadows. As a boy I was taken here a couple of times for garden parties, although we were never invited to swim. Only the tadpoles swim here now, and all the certainty of my childhood is lost.

A man appears out of the mist, in grey and green. He tells me he grew up near the corner of Nod Hill and the Ridgefield Road. He used to work at the Yates farmstand, where my mother would buy us corn. When I left for boarding school, he would have been a little boy.

Homebuyers from the city, he says, as if to the ground. They complain about invasive species killing their trees. But all their precious woods are abandoned pastures. And the little ponds? They ruin everything. So who is to blame? Is it us?

He tries to convince me with his eyes, oblivious to the rain falling on us.

Elizabeth Thomas

The Livin' is Easy

In my dreams
it's always summer—
I'm standing in line at Gold Star Pool
bathing cap and ten cent ticket rolled into my towel,
dancing foot to foot on the hot cement.
Finally, a shrill blast of whistle
and hundreds of rowdy children
tumble through the entrance
like a loose bag of Skittles,
ignoring the shouts of white-nosed lifeguards
while cannonballing into the deep end.
We lived in the house next door to the pool
and treated it as if it were our own.

Always summer—
and I'm peddling my sparkly pink bike
with the butterfly handlebars and banana seat,
the bike I won in a contest on WDRC radio.
Peddling past the towering slide,
the orange spinning merry-go-round,
the picnic tables where kids made lanyards and potholders
with Barbara, the park teacher.
How I lusted after the whistle she wore around her neck.

Always summer—
from lemonade stands under the weeping willow,
to chasing the Good Humor truck
to stir a sky blue bon joy cup into soup.
We'd play hit the bat in the middle of the road
and hide and seek after dark-
Olly olly oxen free.
From Sunday matinees at the Eastwood Theater,

to the Raymond Library where I had a laminated VIP card.
From bike rides to Liggett's Drug Store for 5 cent candy bars
bigger than our fists,
to Seapark's for dungarees and Converse for my brothers,
hot dogs at Augie and Ray's,
warm honey-dipped donuts at Michael's Bakery,
but only if we behaved at church those Sunday mornings
Father Murphy spit fire and brimstone
from the pulpit of St. Christopher's.

Yes, it's always summer—
And we're waiting for the EH Gazette to arrive
to list homerun assignments at Pitkin School
the year we entered 6th grade.
Different teachers, different classmates
and no more rules about girls wearing dresses.
Our young lives were expanding
and we were eager to set aside our mini-skirts and Mary Janes.
Trade them for bell bottoms and desert boots
we purchased surreptitiously with our own money,
saved up from baby sitting and picking tobacco.
We took the city bus into Hartford
then crisscrossed over to the train station
to shop at the UFO Army Surplus store,
this experience so different
from shopping trips with my mom
to Youth Center for my first bra
or Thom McAnns for a new pair of practical shoes.
Instead, we tied on our undercover boots
and took our first steps
beyond   the margins of this page.

Back then,
it was always summer.
And back then,

I could not conceive
how often I would awaken
to dreams of Martin Park,
the grand finale of the July 4th fireworks
fading away.

Robert Cording

For A Friend's Baby

Meehan Road, Woodstock, Connecticut

We've come, neighbors and friends, to this high crown
of field to watch for shooting or falling stars, their name
depending, I guess, on what we bring to this hill.
Our friends have brought their new child and place her,
face up, on a blanket under the night sky. There's the usual
naming of what little we know—Big and Little
Dippers, Cassiopeia, and the stars we think are Perseus—
and then we settle in, timing flights out of Hartford,
a steady pulse of red lights tracing roadmaps
on the sky, this one going West, that one headed out
towards the ocean bustling with its own lanes
of dark activity. Near midnight, and my ten year old son
is on his feet, announcing there's one, and sure enough,
the sky's come alive with its white torch. Soon,
meteors arrive as quick as we can count, streaks of light
too quick to hoard, the profligate sky tossing
a bright profusion of starry coins over our heads
until we're all shouts and smiles. Afterwards, I think
of how the gods loved Perseus and helped him
defeat Medusa. And the story's other half-- the discus
he threw that killed his grandfather by accident,
none of us able to escape the harm we'll give
and receive. Hannah, these are times when stars
are mostly falling and nothing godly visits.
There are no messages in these stoney particles
that burn in our air, nothing occult in this August
night; there are only these meteor showers
that have occurred before, over and over, and will
occur again, and the ordinary moment of our meeting

which so improbably breaks us open each time
into such sweet happiness, as you did, upon your arrival.

Suzannah Dalzell

All Rain Contains A Flood

August, 1955

And there was a lot of rain. Hurricane Connie
stopped by for a visit and before we could change
the sheets Diane showed up, stalled over the Berkshires.

In the wee hours of the 19th the Mad River
hurtled down into Winsted, jumped its banks
bullied its way down main street, then rushed
into the Naugatuck, became a monstrous thing
racing down through mill towns, scraping
factories, stores and homes to rubble.

It slammed into Waterbury where my father
lay recuperating from spine surgery
and where native daughter Rosalind Russell
was being feted—*Before the rains came
I rode in a parade in a white satin dress
being Princess Grace all over the joint.*

By morning thirty-five feet of water
covered the city, eighty-seven people died,
more than fifty coffins had floated away.
Roz escaped—*I directed the driver, 'Go up this hill,
go down that lane. I know this town'*—and Dad
sailed through the ordeal unscathed, happy even,
Scotch being considered a clear liquid in those days.

Over the mountain Mom was a wreck, stuck
in the dark with three small children, phone lines dead.
I don't remember being afraid for I was laser
focused on starting first grade in two weeks.

I do remember our unnamed stream spewing
great curtains of foam and one-story houses
down the road submerged to their eaves.
Bashful and well-behaved Salmon Kill ran wild,
undercut its banks, poured over the low wide cement bridge,
cracked it in half, cutting off access to Lime Rock
and Count Korzybski's Institute for General Semantics.

It took weeks for the water to drain,
fields of flattened corn sparkled in the sunshine,
water lapped at windowsills. A folding Bailey bridge
was brought in. Each day the school bus trundled
across and I'd peer down at the submerged slabs.

Sand, silt, small pebbles dribbled across.
Leaves sank, matted, decayed. Trout
and minnows darted out, snapped at flies.

Natasha S. Garnett

After the Hurricane

Sandy, October 29, 2012

Though the governor silenced the roads
he could not quiet the wind
or our unease

Water jugs, candles, cans, and the news, the news
inevitable disaster for some
for others, fitful sleep to the whipping
and slashing of the trees
gusts loud as desperate engines
and in between
the murmurings of harm

Two days ago we raked the yard
hauling the fall's fallen to the woods
on the straining tarp
and exposing bright and tender green- a late year second spring
what could I do but lie down, open armed
and fill my face with hope and sun?

Today the aftermath– twigs, sticks, branches lie
like litter blown and swept
against the fence of shrubs between our still standing houses
leaves of oak hickory ash birch
and sycamore big as platters scattered wet and yellow
our work cut out for us, the lucky ones

A maple limb knocked the cherub from her perch
rain leaves behind the smell of new dug earth
the highway roar resumes.

John L. Stanizzi

New Autumn

Mouth of the Scantic River,
East Windsor, Connecticut

Colors come now
and the red soil
is fat with rain

Across the river
tatters of cheesecloth
snap in the wind-
torn banners on knuckled poles
where shade-grown had been

Cows stand in early mist
and the slant of the hill reaches up
to where the sun has just begun rise

as I move quietly
through the cool morning, listening
for a butterfly's slow soft applause

Land and Water

Geri Radacsi

Icebreaker on the Connecticut River

The cutter thwacks and punches,
a jolting that deepens below deck
as the crew tries to sleep
between the noise and the motion of falling blows.
Their bones in lost dreams bask easy.
But reality is a haul
miles out to an oil barge, frozen in.
So the captain rams on,
thrusts his vessel's sanity
into ice channels that are groaning,
plagued and narrowing
to make choices straighter.
The hull rears up,
rocks between two brinks,
slides back to try again
until ice squeaks and shivers,
splinters like a lunatic's laugh,
then sags, smashed
by weight or will, slowly, loudly undone.
How quickly new ice rebonds.
On the bridge, the captain wheels
a reasoning of left, right,
caroms over lurches and rolls. He reads
the river's passages—the spectacle
of an eagle and crescent moon gliding the ridge;
carcasses of deer trapped in
thick-ribbed floes, fodder for crows.
Up ahead springs open water.
Who can say why a place resists
freezing—perhaps undercurrents
and a gentler wind conspire to keep
a spirit-shelter built of green.

Marilyn E. Johnston

Connecting and Separating River

River of rivers of Wallace Stevens, local river
of Hugh Ogden, river-vale river of Emily Dickinson,
crossed and re-crossed river
of my ancestors' farms and rituals, crossing
to Glastonbury for Sunday dinner at Grandma's,
crossing to bring Grandma back
to our house for Sunday dinner,
daily crossings to Travelers insurance
and Cigna insurance, and later,
crossing to pick up Mother
to bring her back to our house.
for Sunday dinner. Thousands of crossings—
days seeing you shrunk to your mud banks,
or at high-flood teeming, swallowing trees,
or stalled with white ice slabs grinding south.

I have left you. I have returned to you. I've
ridden your bridges half asleep
on buses to work, dreamed of a lover's
face, glorying over you. I've sought
your sun-glitter from sky-scraper windows,
pedaled my bike to your bridge's center, stared
straight down on your gray, streaming back,
dream river of Wallace Stevens, north-
south winding river of Hugh Ogden, river-
valley river of Emily Dickinson. Stars

reflect on your dark water still
imbibing confluences of childhood brooks,
and home tributaries: Park, Porter, Farmington,
Hockanum, Wash Brook, Deep River, Bride Brook.

We still walk beside you, walk your fields,
and the cliffs above you, ancestral river,
separating, and connecting river,
river of native paddlers, empty river
of Adrien the Dutchman, tradesmen river
of canvas sloops, coveted, battlefield-river
of wrangling American, British, Dutch and Indian.
River of the Great Spirit. Imagined river
of Wallace Stevens, useful river of Samuel Colt,
home-riding river of Hugh Ogden and Emily
Dickinson, river of all my days' loves and losses,
long tidal river of my life.

Natalie Schriefer

At Connecticut River Motocross

A real rider blows by, airborne, tire-spokes
even with my shoulders, my head. Engine
braap-ing, he lands in front of me, spraying
pebbles against my armored chest. It's my first

day on the big track, and maybe it's a victory
that I've stopped flinching at the pebble-clatter,
that I haven't caused a crash. I'm getting good
at staying out of the way, flush right like the slow

lane on the highway—if the highway had ruts
and bumps and riders, boys with unripped
jerseys and race bikes. The bike I'm riding
is too small, borrowed, so I roll the jumps,

suspension heaving. It's all I can do to stay
upright, remember when to stick my foot out
and when to stand, my secondhand boots gritting
against the pegs as another rider streaks by,

another boy. I'm the only girl here, and I don't know
if that's a victory or a failure—and if it is, whose.
All I know is that I want to be those boys.
I want their instinct, their skill, their power.

Every hour the irrigation turns on, and the boys
exit for a coaching break, a snack, gas,
to change into a fresh shirt or towel off their hair,
slick with sweat. I stay. I'm no racer but I pin

the accelerator open, roll another jump. Cold jets
of water arc against my helmet, spilling from
my visor to my thighs, and when I crest the big hill,
for a moment I feel it: the dirt infinite, open, and mine.

Gwen North Reiss

West Rock

Yesterday I drove through my old neighborhood
near the foot of West Rock. I wanted to take
a photo of the cliff side, capture rooftops
and the rock-loving trees running up that late
Triassic rift where once basalt lava flooded in—
while North America continued to rip itself away
from Eurasia and Africa, and the ground tilted up,
sediment eroding to reveal the igneous rock,
a sheer face of earth-combed striations
scraped by the glacier into vertical ridges
red with iron, a towering underworld
that once here could never slip back—and settled
over generations of us, catching the light
as only a broken thing can do.

Joan Hofmann

At Powder Hollow Trail

Scantic River State Park, Enfield, Connecticut

I take the rubbled path from the parking lot,
meander down to the river, hear its spry gurgle
long before I see it—rushing over the glistened rocks.

I'm in the thrall of dragonflies. I hold back, try not
to go in the water though I'm drawn to it. To feel its
forested coolness. I stand still where lather laces shoreline,

watch the whoosh and imagine riding it …
put out of my mind the stuffed drawers at home,
the boiling ocean, my family fractured by loss.

In the ether of the stream, let those recurring thoughts
and burdensome intrusions evaporate. Instead,
a turtle's shell with its patterned scutes, a shrill

of blackbird in the understory, a shimmer of insect noise.
And, too, I'm surrounded by carnage of predation,
always the code of the saplinged and treed woodlands.

I seek the peace of life's cycle, even with its predicted loss:
you're never far from death. A meander in the woods
proves it. Now a whip of light so substantial

illuminates a narrow rocky span where water
barely trickles through. I feel a switch in my breath,
Flesh quivers. My heart skips. I fall heavy into the day's arms.

Tom Nicotera

Thanksgiving at Great Pond, Sunset

Great Pond State Forest, Simsbury, Connecticut

Red spots against the dark swampy woods—
winterberry thriving everywhere, their berries
hung like rubies along slender arms springing from water.
The long pond's water is turning gray
but along the far shore sun kindles the trees with yellow fire.
The western side's already darkened,
the eastern side is glowing brightly.

Everything is patterned. These are not just
trees and water and rocks but lines and angles,
the thrusting perpendicular vernacular of trees,
the horizontal dialectics of rippling waters and stolid rocks,
a language of shape and color, a pronouncement
of there and here and now
in a poetry unmistakable to the eye.

Then the wind stirs
and the incendiary candelabras of trees flare
then sway and swirl and swish
in movements more graceful than any dancers I've seen.
The brilliant greens of pines, the rusted orange of oaks,
brush a sky turned magenta from a gaudy blue,
a few thin layers of clouds skirting above like skilled skaters.

A formation of geese suddenly flies above,
their prior distant honks a musical forewarning
of their easeful entrance to waiting waters.
I look up to see the geese overhead, their white bellies
illuminated from the sun's last glowing
like so many lanterns in the sky soaring
till they softly land in lake water

with a whoosh and a hush
and a rhythmic rippling of the twilight-grey surface.
A dialogue of muted honks subdues the quiet air
till all are still and water resumes its dominance of peace.

I cannot move, so numbed am I from miracles.
The sun's now gone. As twilight settles
on the darkening woods, the living lights of trees
slowly snuffed, pond water turning
from film of grey to opaque black,

I know I must move on before trail disappears
and I am lost. It's then I realize that God
is not separate from this, nor did God make this
wild and wayfaring cosmos from some lofty perch.
God is every flaring branch, every rainstorm,
every star spinning for a million years,
every possum snuffling through the woods,
every wild goose settling for the night,
every artist's vision nature paints and sculpts
just by being there.

I give thanks that for this one day, this brief walk,
I was given so much, and I walk
into the encumbering darkness
light in step, light in vision, light inside.

Marjorie Maddox

Walking the Prayer Labyrinth in Spring

Mercy by the Sea Retreat Center

If mourn is what you do,
these tended rows open the throats
of those who weep. In spring, the path
turns always toward what you need.

These rows open into birdsong. The throat
opens, too. Follow where the hedge
turns toward what you need. It's spring;
at the center is calm, the breeze a mere hum.

Open to the chants of spring. Follow where
their mantras take you. If song is what you need,
hum with the breeze till your center is calm.
Follow where the hedge opens notes.

Its mantra will take you to song. What you need is
here, steps moving forwards in spring.
Follow where the hedge opens notes
into prayer, the sister of sorrow and joy.

Here, steps move forward in spring.
These rows of green open the throat
to prayer, sister of joy and sorrow.
Turn always toward what you need.

This tended labyrinth opens the throat
of those who weep and sing. It's spring;
follow the green this path gives
if pray is what you do.

Victoria Nordgren

Towards Greenwich Point

i. The Connecticut Sound Shore at Greenwich Point

Rivers mutter in rivulets,
clear waters enter the salt of the Sound
and the estuarial ridges dissolve.

What absences of soul that I feel
can be tended to where the ocean booms
and the sky divulges its illuminations.

I am a gathering of elegies
listening for the sluice in the rocks,
underwater bells of the drowned shoreline.

Fossils of ferns and fishbones
can be found in the sediment,
waves against a land inconstant and shifting.

The Sound is not the open Atlantic,
but a great circulation of waters
emptying into the ocean and churned by the tides.

Fields of geese take flight,
like longing arising. They straighten
their necks and fly northwards.

Morning's land, though shadowed,
disperses my shadows and I am inflamed
with devotion for this meeting of waters.

Sometimes when the ocean is mercury-still,
I can feel its gentle tremble
like upturned palms held open in my lap.

ii. Elizabeth Fones Winthrop Feake Hallett (1610 - 1673)—Elizabeth's
Neck

I imagine the ocean journey from England remains long in her bones.

*My family's ship Lyon has landed in the colonies of New England
and New Netherlands. It is November 1631. I have carried Martha,
my fatherless babe, the whole way in my arms. My husband, Winthrop,
travelled before me and has died here, drowned.*

I imagine the wilderness she encounters, wild chasms of beauty.

*My uncle, Governor Winthrop of the Massachusetts Bay Colony,
pledges me to a wealthy landowner, Feake. We marry on a gray
New World morning and acquire a great plot of land near the ocean.
I bear him five children, while he grows troubled in mind.*

I imagine the names that she links to her own as shells strung from a
cord.

*The wars of men are constant—the Pequot and the Mohegan, the Dutch,
and the English, over trading routes and lands. Smallpox and slaughter
have decimated the tribes, and a great storm strikes the colonies in 1635
with winds and waves that destroy property and kill people.*

I imagine her constant prayers for her children and for peace.

*Feake has abandoned our family, and I marry again, my third husband,
Hallett. I bear him two sons, and acquire, in my own name, the lands
that the Siwanoy call Monakewego—"Shining Sands."
I have named it "Elizabeth's Neck."*

I imagine her standing on the southwest promontory
of the lands that now bear her name, Elizabeth's Neck.
What power has she known but from husbands and lands,
and does she wonder if the lands know of their captivity?

Dusk falls over her oceanside wilderness. It smells of juniper
and brine. Clouds hasten, indigo-violet in the autumn sky.
She incants the prayers of her ocean voyage: *"O God, let the waters
under heaven be gathered into one place, and let dry land appear."*

iii. Glacial Time

    Before Elizabeth and Feake
    Before Petuquapaen and Groenwits
    Before the Siwanoy, and the Dutch, and the English
    Before Monakewego
    Before Quinnehtukqut

This angled island, this estuarial shoreline, was a domain of ice.

The till and drift of glacial leavings are scattered
through Connecticut's woodlands, as if a creature
had been birthed from the rock and escaped whole.

Grooves and striae in the bedrock, boulders top-tilted
and dropped, stones gathered and stacked
trail through the trees like squirrel smoke.

The weight of the great ice layer pressed down
upon the land, stifled the ocean, and hoarded
the cold for more than 14,000 years.

Glacial time is not ours. It is an evolutionary sloth,
dragging its weight over droplets of melt,
splitting rock and amassing the pieces.

In the lowlands between tree-covered hills
when the leaf-layered earth is both sodden and frozen,
when drafts of air are full of snow-melt chill, you can feel

ghost glaciers whisper against your throat, "I am gone and so shall you
follow."

Antoinette Brim-Bell

Upon Viewing Simmons' *Eight Mile River Reflections*

It's a joy to be subtracted from the world. —Gary Young

Eight Mile River needs no audience.
It shushes creation—
claps hard against the rocks.
It is its own call and response.

Let the sunlight-soaked stones
skip across this canvas
where amethyst lay with emerald
and interspersed colorways become
thoroughfares where blues
enter into rivulets of jazz.

Confluence: is where
the painter's brush meets the light
this torrential river has polished
into smooth shards to be placed
atop mosaic-petalled sprays
chromed into mirrored infinity.

We are voyeurs—
an unwelcome convergence of wonder and worry.

Leave the river to sleep in its deep shadows,
where brushstrokes turn touchstones,
while water-soaked air smudges
liquid graphite into an open palm
that holds up the whole
Eight Mile River.

Melissa Studdard

Shhhhh, said the waves, saving language for themselves

It's that time of evening when light
visits only in streaks and flashes. The seagull
blinks like a cursor in the sky, and I
walk beneath her
contemplating what to type. The first time
light touched water here, a jellyfish
caught it in her bell and decided
the shoreline was a sentence
that would never end. Each wave
opened a portal to a smaller
wave where an undersea alphabet
mixed and remixed, spilling out to sea.
East Haven is not beautiful, people say,
not like the rest of the state. But
as often as the waves
visit, they must disagree. In their
postcards to the ocean
the waves write *Next Service 12 Miles,*
Keep Driving, like I will report
this place as industrial parks and donut shops
so I can keep walking on this beach
where saltwater holds the secrets I seek,
where my name is the only word
traced daily in the sand.

Brad Davis

On the Way to Putnam

Were you to tell him how,
in late summer's

westering light,
his yellow cornfields and,

toward the middle,
that lone, misshapen tree

had become your very own
Serengeti, complete

with buzzards
ascending and descending

upon some bloated corpse,
likely a wildebeest,

Mr. Amaral, a businessman,
would nod politely.

Margaret Gibson

Flood Plain, Lit and Shadowed by Sun and Clouds

The Wood Parcel, Great Meadows Conservation Trust
Glastonbury, Connecticut

Skeow! yelps the green heron
as it lifts from a limb of bitternut
hickory—*Now!*

Now also, the sound of a tractor nearby
in the corn harvest.
Now, the crunch of my boots

on the patchy gravel and dirt trail
that weaves past
a slump of earth where a house once

in the 18th century
was, before it was razed to make way
for a highway—

this whoosh on the edge of stillness.

Time is a flood plain, a cornfield,
a house, a swamp—
but whoever

named it "Fearful Swamp" was
not a Wangunk.
They wove cattail mats,

ate shoots and roots, fished river,
brook, and cove.
They transformed plants

into medicine. Time is the tractor
uncovering their bones
while planting seed corn.

Time is sedge grass, swamp
meadow, a brook
lit and shadowed in sun.

Beaver Brook was redirected.
It was common once,
this draining of the flood plains

for corn fields, turf farms, suburbs,
highways—
transforming meander into linear.

Tell me, where, where exactly,
is the remnant flood plain,
swamp, and forest now?

Perhaps you can find it, if
with your whole
body in sunlight and shadow,

you stand still (just breathe)
and read the land
long enough to sense the covenant

that links sycamore, migrant
oriole, corn farmer,
native pharmacist, alluvial silts,

arrow root, and black willow, bone,
seed, root, and canopy
into one flooding

of water wind sunlight earth.
Tell me, why would you
want to alter that covenant?

Time is a flood plain.

Time is also a young doe, struck
alongside the concrete
traffic barrier, center lane, Route 3.

Looking Back

Pat Murphy McClelland

Inner City

New Haven, Connecticut

Cicadas sing approaching heat
the peddler Bellen passes by
his dry bleached wood cart
sighs in the sun; veined leather
reins pull taut, the sluggish horse
halts, disturbing rosy stacks
of ripened fruit in the shade
of green and orange canvas
wedges of umbrella citrus
looking edible, delicious.

Noon: mothers dole out chores.
Mrs. Margolis rules her store
from the oil-stained butcher
block where smoked white fish
lies, gold skin shimmering isinglass;
flaked white flesh awaits dividing
slashes of her keen-edged knife.
In the kosher bakery on Legion
Jewish rye loaves tumble through the slicer
amber heels blazoned with the union label.

Afternoons the ice man comes
carrying blocks of crystal ice
leaking water on leather
spread across his shoulder
black galoshes squeak
to the silver-latched white chest
where cod liver oil and lemon Jello
 share a shelf with icebox cake
honey grahams interlaced with chocolate pudding.

Black iron tongs slide the smoking load
into a small dark square of frozen space.

Dusk falls, games of Spud
dominate the street, jurisdiction
of post-war kids. A knife grinder
peddles into view on a rusty
metal trike-like apparatus
the circle spins, sparks fly
urgent cries cut through
soft silk summer-evening air:
"Scissors, knives whetted cheap."
The wheel hones as mother
gossip mixes in the buzz.

Girls in shorts sit on stoops
trading picture cards they keep
 in red and gold silver-lined chests
that once held Swee-Touch-Nee tea
black flecks and dusty scent
tarry under domed lids
inscribed with Gothic script.

On the western wall
of Goldstein's drugstore
pink rubber Spalding balls
ruddy in the setting sun
bounce off coral brick
in a game of Spanish
sing-song voices ricochet
up and down the block—
"A my name is Alice"
mixes with the clicks
of tiger-striped agates—
glass against macadam—
with boasts of bossy boys

showing off in "Mother May I."

Night comes to cool down
the street by soft degrees.
Dark green shades drawn
kids long gone to bed
the domain of stoop now
passes on to parents.
Radios drone.
The deeds of Churchill and Truman
trickle through mesh screens
charged with foiling mosquitoes.
Beams of crescent moon
find holes in the shade.
I smell gin and lemon, Camels, sweat,
and the sweet of sun-dried sheets.

Chris Abbate

Home Run

I hit a home run off him once that they are still looking for,
my father says of Steve Dalkowski,
the fastest pitcher the Greater Hartford Twilight League
had ever seen. Maybe the fastest of all time
if radar guns had existed in the late 1950's.
As unpredictable as lightning, walked
almost as many batters as he struck out.
A real son of a gun, my father says,
seeing how he had dodged
a ball Dalkowski aimed at his head
before hitting that homer the very next pitch.

He chokes up talking about it now,
a faraway look in his eyes, surveying
the arc of his life – how he stopped
playing baseball so he could make a living,
raise a family rather than chase a dream.
It's as if he is trying to recapture a part of himself
he lost like the ball he hit off Dalkowski that day—
launched from my father's bat, still rising, I imagine,
over the South End of Hartford, the Colt firearms
factory and its heavenly blue dome
speckled with stars.

Deborah Howard

East Rock Park, 1978

Walking past my old house,
I remember what had been forgotten—
how Peter, David, Carl, and I
would saunter down Eagle Street
until we reached the park.
Tarps wound around Blake Field
so people would pay,
but we always found a way in.
There was a crowd
every night of the week—
Perry Flowers commanded second base,
Gary Bello defended the hole,
and Pat Paulsen threw cannons
from the outfield
in the white, green, and blue
of the New England Pilgrims.
At ten years old
our first jobs were fetching balls,
lining the fields,
and helping Tony
in the concession stand.
We didn't earn much,
but five dollars was enough
for pizza and ice cream
down at Clarks after the game.
Once we even traveled
with the team to Shea Stadium.
It was Lee Mazzilli Day—
complete with a souvenir bat.
I've lost the bat,
Peter and Carl have passed away,
and I don't know what happened to Dave—

but I can still hear
the roar from the stands
stirring in the summer breeze.

Tony Fusco

The Last Day of School

Savin Rock Amusement Park, West Haven, Connecticut 1850-1965

Penny rolls clenched in our hands
we carefully balance stepping down
the large steps of the bus, without

holding on. Smells intrude, popcorn,
French fries, hotdogs and that underlying
hint of something else,

seaweed cooking in its stew of salt water,
overdone yesterday-- a scent like nowhere
else in the world. Our coins scrounged and saved

throughout the long winter—stored in piggy
banks and empty *ZaRex* glass juice jars
shaped like Abe Lincoln, with a slot in his

top hat. In the distance we hear three clangs
in rapid succession, the carousel house
sharing space with the penny arcade where

nothing costs a penny anymore, our destination.
My father leads, but we have memorized the way
and do not venture ahead into the crowd with

all the people in the street dazed in the heat
of the place as if staggering. It is so unusual to
not dodge cars or trucks; it is a street for people

The pavement is sticky underfoot scavenger
gulls fish through feet and litter
for a morsel, battling among themselves for

a clam strip or a dropped crinkle cut fry. My
sister and I stay close sifting into the place,
through the press of people less each year. We

navigate between hips and legs, around hand-
holders and cotton candy obstacles, anxious
stopping at a booth, a game of chance so rare

for dad, shooting the cracking twenty-two
caliber miniature bullets at clay pipes and ducks.
I take a shot, happier to pocket the small brass

casing, a prize without having to pay for it.
This is not the routine, the circuit we have come
to know by rote of traversing the park in a given order:

First the flying horses, the bumper cars, the Skeeball,
finally crossing the street to avoid the scary
Laff in the Dark to arrive at the kiddy rides

and if weather threatened, the fun house,
Peter Frank's, with the moving steps,
the rolling barrel and the great slide, where

packaged into a burlap sack kids slid the slick metal
drop in seconds to crash into the padded wall at the
bottom. I was too afraid of height and burns to ride,

each year managing another couple of more dizzy
steps closer to the top, bag in hand to the urging
of my father and sister. Maybe next time, next

season. We did not waste money on food with
dinner waiting at home, maybe one snack or treat
before the end, a *dip-topped* soft ice cream cone or

a box of popcorn, one half to eat and one half
for the pigeons on the green while waiting for
our transfer between buses. Our day usually ending

with a few cents in our pockets and almost
enough Skeeball tickets for a prize, if we didn't
lose them by next year, and we remembered

to bring them next year and if we didn't read
the signs that were posted everywhere and
on the rickety roller coaster and Mill Chute

or know what the word *redevelopment* meant
or *condemned* or even that there might not be
a Rock to return to next year or any year, ever again.

Eva M. Schlesinger

Remembering A Connecticut Childhood

I'm thinking about the woods
across from our house
the boulder I climbed on to survey the trees
the leaves, brown and wet, on the ground
the Black Botanical Gardens
with a huge hill for sledding
In winter I whooshed just inches away from
the tadpole pond covered with cracked ice
In summer I visited the tadpoles
the frogs they became
the murky water
I lay on a pine needle floor among evergreens
I walked on trails as familiar as my own backyard in the Arboretum
I crunched through autumn leaves, past skunk cabbage,
to catch a glimpse of the frogs that leapt off their lily pads
the turtles that sunned on stones
and slipped off to paddle to larger rocks
I sat waiting on a stone wall
Walks at Harkness Park, barefoot in summer grass
watching gulls, osprey, red-winged blackbirds
Visits to the gardens
the coy goldfish in the dank little pool–
now they're just Koi
I stooped under feathery boughs,
stepping on a stone path that led to lilies of the valley,
wandering by the beach, that long stretch of water
I long for it, that water,
those waves, that ocean
I long for the smell of that sea

Elizabeth Poliner

East Hampton, Connecticut 1977

The bells I didn't hear
were those of our own bell factories.

Downtown, the best business
no longer came to Clark's Gifts & Jewelry,

but to Cumberland Farms and the package store,
a decline as telling as the two brick warehouses,

windows smashed, proof of how we hadn't produced
even one bell in twenty years. Still,

*We are the Bellringers, the mighty
mighty Bellringers!* we cried on Friday nights

at high school basketball games, our chants rising
as if to put the spirits of the past

back to work, if only to change the score
underneath the word HOME. Though our namesake,

the region's sappiest, made us feel more or less
like ding-a-lings, we Bellringers

didn't know how to reach for a better name.
After the game, angry boys, my classmates,

called our town *Goon City.*
Fucking Goon City. Generally, East Hampton

was a quiet place. Except on Friday nights,
after lost games, when the hurt spirits

of the living Bellringers sounded.

Michaela Godding

the Litchfield House

      was often dark
but great at keeping
the heat in

every time it snowed
the family would end
      up above the ceiling
shoveling the weight off
so the roof wouldn't
cave in

the backyard would watch
as the father would taunt
his daughter   to jump
into the large pile leftover
from all the emptying

zipped up in her too small
jacket she would bite her lip
and ask the angels to remake her
the kind of kid   brave enough
to jump off a roof

one day   the deer   the axe
the gaze of raccoons   all stilled
and she finally leapt   brave
ankle twisted

her father   still
shoveling had missed   the leap
and the snow   kept coming

Garrett Phelan

Confirmation

Early, with little money, we'd gather at the corner,
slip into Maxwell Drugs on Farmington Avenue
and climb onto the red and silver stools,
order a Cherry Coke, light up a Lucky Strike
and inhale deeply.

Sometimes, bored, we'd exhale
into our straw submerged in the cherry-Coke
and watch the bubbles burst with cigarette smoke.
Soon, we divide into pairs, stick out our thumbs

on North Main Street and hitchhike to Barkhamsted
to swim across the huge reservoir,
climb the cliff walls, or dive from tree limbs—
to dare ourselves to be indestructible.

Once on the way home the driver of the car
hit 110mph on Rte. 44 to impress us.
We laughed. We got out at Bishop's Corner,
lit our cigarettes and inhaled. When we returned,

we put one foot up against the wall of Maxwell Drugs,
leaned back, and exhaled, happy with who we were.

Glinda Johnson-Medland

Ode to Connecticut

I was born where the white birches
huddle like cattle
against a winter storm
and many of the mountains on the Mohawk Trail are
more stone than dirt.

Connecticut.
Where stories of The Leatherman
and young boys taken
in the cantankerous currents of the Housatonic River,
are served up with warm corn fish stew
and biscuits.
I crossed railroad trestles over the Naugatuck River with nothing more
than raw courage and my brother's hand.
I swam in spring-fed lakes,
dove into dark icy waters and imagined dragons in cold lairs
licking my toes.
Wintergreen still grows on the high mountains there.
The graves of my distant family
are under the shade of massive pine trees
that whisper secrets in the wind.
Secrets of a young boy killed sledding,
a civil war soldier that never returned home,
my mother's mother's mother who lost her inheritance for marrying a
          hunter and a trapper
but found love instead.
When the ground holds your loved ones,
you hold that soil dear.

Connecticut, Connecticut.
The paradise that was mine:
Pink Lady's slippers,

Star-nosed moles in the middle of winter,
blackberries in summer,
puffballs in fall,
Short-tailed weasels,
Long-tailed mink.
Waterfalls across the highway.
Winter skating with bonfires on black ice.
Swimming in the creek.
Hot dogs eaten raw.
Lucky rabbit paws.

Connecticut, Connecticut, Connecticut
My name is carved on a tree somewhere
that is probably in somebody's lawn.
The field that held the ponies,
gone now beneath the sod of manicured yards.
Why did I have to grow this old to want what I already had?
I am gone too long,
gone long,
too long
to return to my childhood home.

Judith H. Montgomery

Eden

Route 7 north shimmies like a spine
   of moon, winds through fields flooded

out of Housatonic's rush, past the slumped
   garage where yellow busses drowsed through

grammar school, the town hall where I signed
   my life away to wed . . . The steering

wheel compasses an arc of light as I
   hang west to catch 341, let the steel

bones of the bridge sing each tire awake
   above trout's silver fin. The crew house waits

below for oarlift, and coxswain's dawn rouse—
   the chapel tower anchors its still bells.

Can anyone say how land and water,
   road and mark, seize the exiled heart?

Beyond the dashboard clock, the lambing
   pasture, barn's loom—a farmhouse window

holds its wait-up light. Beneath a strew
   of stars, the white-frame house that once

cradled my sky-painted room: I cut
   my lights, set the brake, hesitate—

one hundred rowdy peepers charge the night—
   then feel my way along the gravel path

that crooks a curve where once it traveled
    true. I reach the stoop—*should I have called ?*—

new brass latches shut the kitchen door . . .
    but still it swings on sweet hinges: hot

apples, sugar, nutmeg, lard. The cocker,
    gray-muzzled now, barks, and clicks her nails

across the shoe-smooth floor. *Home,* I call
    at last. I rub her honey coat. *I'm home.*

Contributors Notes

Chris Abbate has published two collections of poetry, *Talk About God* (Main Street Rag, 2017) and *Words for Flying* (FutureCycle Press, 2022). Visit him at chrisabbate.com.

About his poems, he says: My father was in attendance on the day of the Hartford Circus Fire. He was five years old. He attributes his surviving the fire to his own father's ability to pull strings to get front row seats.

My father played baseball in the Greater Hartford Twilight League in the 1950's and played with many players who went on to the majors. This story about him hitting a home run against the fastest pitcher the game may have ever seen is one of his, and my, favorites.

Elizabeth Alexander decorated poet, educator, memoirist, scholar, and cultural advocate—is president of The Andrew W. Mellon Foundation, the nation's largest funder in arts and culture, and humanities in higher education. Dr. Alexander has held distinguished professorships at Smith College, Columbia University, and Yale University, where she taught for 15 years and chaired the African American Studies Department. She is Chancellor Emeritus of the Academy of American Poets, a member of the American Academy of Arts and Sciences, serves on the Pulitzer Prize Board, and co-designed the Art for Justice Fund. Notably, Alexander composed and delivered "Praise Song for the Day" for the 2009 inauguration of President Barack Obama, and is author or co-author of fourteen books. Her book of poems, *American Sublime*, was a finalist for the Pulitzer Prize in Poetry in 2006, and her memoir, *The Light of the World*, was a finalist for the Pulitzer Prize in Biography in 2015.

"Allegiance" is part of a collection of poems about Prudence Crandall and her students, a collaborative project between Elizabeth Alexander and Marilyn Nelson. Crandall opened her school to young women of color early in the 1800s. Persecution from white citizens caused the school to close.

Dennis Barone, Professor Emeritus in English and American Studies at the University of Saint Joseph, has lived near Elizabeth Park for forty years. Among his many books are *Far-Dale: New and Selected Poems* and *Beyond Memory: Italian Protestants in Italy and America*. He is the poetry editor for *The Wallace Stevens Journal*.

Sheryll Bedingfield is the author of three poetry collections: *Transitions and Transformations, The Clattering: Voices from old Forfarshire, Scotland* and *In the Dream You Wore Your Yellow Leaves*. Sherri did the artwork on the covers for all three.

About her poem, she says: Meeting a "White Rose" at Elizabeth Park in the summer sunlight and imagining a conversation with the attentive blossom gave me a real joy. I love that I feel such connections with nature.

Sarah Blanchard: Woodstock's early history comprises two threads: one from the long-established indigenous Nipmucs; the other from English settlers who arrived in 1674 with Reverend John Eliot, who established his largest "Indian Praying Town" (Qabbaquassett) near Woodstock Hill. In 1675, when King Philip's War erupted, the Nipmuc tribe was decimated—despite their alliance with colonists.

Visiting cemeteries and native burial mounds, I was struck by how both groups made good use of the abundant granite and fieldstone.

Antoinette Brim-Bell, Connecticut's 8th State Poet Laureate (2022 - 2025), is the author of three full-length poetry collections: *These Women You Gave Me, Icarus in Love*, and *Psalm of the Sunflower*. She is a Cave Canem Foundation Fellow and an alumna of Voices of Our Nations Arts Foundation (VONA). Brim-Bell was nominated for the Pushcart Prize twice, for poetry and essay.

Havi Brouillard: This poem was created this summer, when over the course of a few months my family and I would hear random horns that sounded like a train coming from the direction of the old railroad turned walking trail in Vernon. I never figured out where the noises were actually coming from, but it made a fun story, and it made me feel more connected to this neighborhood I've lived in my entire life.

Kevin Carey calls himself an undocumented amateur in the world of MFAs, driven to write for pleasure, and purge. He enjoys sharing his work at readings. It is rewarding to read a piece to others, gage reactions. A Spanish proverb says, that if one wishes to be remembered, there are three paths: 1) be a parent, 2) plant a tree, 3) create art. As a confirmed bachelor, allergic to so many pollens, only the third option remains.

Brian Clements: My wife, Abbey, survived the shooting at Sandy Hook, and for a year and a half afterwards I had a total writing block from the weight of grief. Then one day I had a stark memory of dropping off my son at Sandy Hook and while waiting in the drop-off line seeing a great horned owl staring down at us from a tree beside the school, maybe fifty feet from the car. This poem rose from that memory.

William Conlon received his MFA in Creative Writing at Southern Connecticut State University in May 2023. He previously earned his B.A. degree in liberal studies at SCSU. His chapbook, *Speaking of the Sixties in Verse*, was published in April 2021 by Flying Horse Press and his story collection, *Missing All the Stars*, by KDP in September 2025. Bill lives with his wife, Debbi, near the beach in West Haven, Connecticut.

Ginny Connors: In Twain's day, Hartford was a bustling center of publishing, and host to many fine writers and intellectuals. Harriet Beecher Stowe was a neighbor of the Clemens. The Mark Twain House itself still seems to burst with stories: of the man, his family, his fascinating friends, and the books written and read there. When his daughters were young, Twain would tell them a different story every evening, incorporating the objects on the fireplace mantel in the library.

Robert Cording has published ten collections of poems, the most recent of which is *In the Unwalled City* (Slant, 2022). Two new books, *What's Possible: New and Selected Poems* and *Taking the Shadows Apart* are forthcoming from Slant. He has won three Pushcart Prizes in poetry, and his poems have appeared in publications such as the *Georgia Review, Southern Review, 32 Poems, Hudson Review, Kenyon Review, Image, The Sun, The Common, Agni, New Ohio Review, Orion,* and *Best American Poetry, 2018.*

Suzannah Dalzell: Hurricanes Connie and Diane show up on the National Hurricane Center's list of "Hurricanes in History" and are always mentioned together. I moved away from Connecticut fifty-plus years ago, but memories of those storms came pouring back in when reading about the devastation Hurricane Helene caused in North Carolina's western Appalachian region. I currently live on Whidbey Island north of Seattle, Washington.

Brad Davis is a Canadian American living in Putnam, Connecticut. His most recent poetry collection is *On the Way to Putnam.*

 "Among Erratics" grew out of a deep fascination with the large boulders left here and there in northeastern Connecticut ten thousand years ago by the receding glacier. "On the Way to Putnam" reflects upon a picturesque farm property between Pomfret and Putnam in Connecticut's Quiet Corner, a property once owned by the Amaral family.

Cortney Davis is the author of five poetry collections, three award winning memoirs, and co-editor of three anthologies of creative writing by nurses. Honors include an NEA Poetry Grant, two Center for the Book Awards, and three CT Commission on the Arts Poetry Grants. Her poems have appeared in *Last Stanza, Poetry, Hanging Loose, CALYX, Witness, Rattle, The Sun,* and other journals and anthologies. Cortney is Poet Laureate Emerita of Bethel, Connecticut.

William Derge's poems have appeared in *Negative Capability*, *The Bridge*, *Artful Dodge*, and many other publications. He is the winner of the 2010 Knightsbridge Prize judged by Donald Hall and has been nominated for a Pushcart Prize. He is a winner of the Rainmaker Award judged by Marge Piercy. He has been awarded a grant by the Maryland State Arts Council.

Ralph Earle grew up in Wilton, Connecticut and currently lives in North Carolina. His two poetry collections are *Everything You Love is New* (Redhawk Publications) and *The Way the Rain Works* (Sable Books). His poems have appeared in *The Sun, Sufi Journal, Carolina Quarterly*, and elsewhere. He meditates daily and believes that simple, loving practices will see us through.

Adele Evershed is a Welsh writer and poet living in Connecticut. Her work has appeared in Poetry *Wales, Modern Haiku, Contemporary Haibun Online, Flashflood, Atrium*, and *Literary Mama*. She is the author of two poetry collections, *Turbulence in Small Spaces* (Finishing Line Press) and *The Brink of Silence* (Bottlecap Press), with a third, *In the Belly of the Wail*, forthcoming from Querencia Press. She has also published novellas-in-flash and a short story collection.

Gretchen Fletcher: I'm a Florida girl, but my in-laws lived in Manchester, Connecticut, where we often visited them. Such a contrast between the trees there and the palm trees here! Many of my poems about Florida are in one of my chapbooks, *The Scent of Oranges*. I was a winner in the Poetry Society of America's Bright Lights, Big Verse competition and read my winning poem in Times Square while being projected on the Jumbotron.

Tony Fusco is a past Poet Laureate of the City of West Haven. He has an MA in Creative Writing from Southern Connecticut State University. He has served as President of the Connecticut Poetry Society. Fusco's work has appeared in many publications including *Connecticut Review, Louisiana Literature, the Red Rock Review, The South Carolina Review, Rattle, The Paterson Review*, and over 90 journals and anthologies. He is the author of seven books of poetry.

Natasha Garnett earned a degree in English from Dartmouth College. She writes snail mail to friends, picture books, and poetry. Her work has appeared in *River Walk Journal, Oak Bend Review, Toasted Cheese Literary Journal, Here: a poetry journal, McNeese Review*, and *DASH Literary Journal*. Given more space, she would wax poetic about Jeffrey, rugby, Bolivia, Venezuela, daughters, walking in the woods, biking up hills, and owls. San Francisco is Garnett's birthplace, but Connecticut is her home.

Fred Gerhard: "My Father Teaches Me to Drive the Trolley" is a true story. Fred Gerhard and his father are now motormen at the Shoreline Trolley Museum in East Haven, Connecticut. The author of *Drifting to "Hello,"* he has had poems in *BlazeVOX, Friends Journal*, and other magazines. An editor for *Quabbin Quills*, he also runs the annual *Poetry on the Rails* reading, trolley excursion, and open mic at the Shoreline Trolley Museum every September. Visit FredGerhard.com

Margaret Gibson, Connecticut State Poet Laureate (2019-2022) has published 14 books of poems with LSU Press. She lives in Preston, Connecticut.

After poet David Leff died, I was assigned to walk the Wood Parcel in Glastonbury, Connecticut for him. I wrote the poem for *Writing the Land*, a project that celebrates conserved land. This poem is dedicated to David. Walking the Wood Parcel, reading the land, is like walking back into time and Connecticut history.

D. Walsh Gilbert lives in Farmington, Connecticut on a former sheep farm in the original lands of the Tunxis peoples. A dual citizen with the Republic of Ireland, she has written three Irish historical-fiction stories-in-verse—*Finches in Kilmainham, Misneach,* and *From the Altar of the Land* (Grayson Books, 2024/25) as well as several other chapbooks. She helps to bring readers to the Riverwood Poetry Series and is associate editor of *Connecticut River Review.*

Michaela Godding, born and raised in Connecticut, is currently a Poetry MFA candidate at George Mason University. She is the author of a chapbook, *dwelling.* Her debut full collection, *The Year Our Grandmothers Died,* will be released in February 2026. Follow her on her instagram, @michaelagodding.

I moved and lived at eight different addresses while living in Connecticut. The years I lived in Litchfield I remember being particularly cold, both outside and personally, and this poem was my attempt at capturing the loud silence and isolation that came with being in a family with no choice but to dig ourselves out of the snow.

José B. González: José B. González is the author of *Toys Made of Rock, When Love Was Reels* and the upcoming collection, *Tongue Wrapped in Twine* (FlowerSong Press 2026).

"Along Mystic's Pequot Avenue" is an affirmation of a history that is often ignored in Connecticut, especially in tourist-centered areas. The poem is intended to encourage readers to travel physically beyond those areas in order to get a fuller sense of what is often viewed as beautiful but rarely seen as veiled, and to recognize how Indigenous populations have been a pivotal part of the state's existence.

Anne Hampford: The forests of Easton have delighted and inspired me for decades—each season in different garb, with new stories. A warm weather woman, I resist winter and its cold until the first snow arrives and invites me into the particular quiet it creates in the woods.

Dolores Hayden's poems have appeared in *Poetry*, *Kenyon Review*, and *The Best American Poetry*. *Exuberance* (Red Hen Press) is her most recent collection. She is Professor Emerita of Architecture, Urbanism, and American Studies at Yale.

I wrote *Building Suburbia: Green Fields and Urban Growth* (Pantheon) during the years when I commuted between downtown New Haven and Guilford, so I deployed suburban landscape history to frame the geography of widowhood, going home to an empty house.

Ruth Hoberman: "In Abeyance": In July, 2019, my husband and I rented a small apartment in downtown New Haven to be near our daughter and son-in-law and their three-year-old daughter. I loved New Haven's strange juxtapositions: of grittiness and elegance, of seascape and urban density. So many seagulls! So many ads for lawyers!

"With my Granddaughter at the Peabody Museum": The Peabody Museum was an ideal spot for entertaining a three-year-old. The long dark corridors were rarely crowded, and the spot-lit dioramas were magical. It did occur to me, though, that natural history museums are disturbing places if you think too hard about them.

Joan Hofmann: "At Powder Hollow Trail" is part of an important book celebrating the place, time, and history of the Connecticut River through prose, poetry and photography: *Writing the Land: The Connecticut River*. Joan Hofmann often chooses to write of the natural world, particularly Connecticut and often with a focus on the environs of and near Collinsville on the Farmington River. To hear her read "At Powder Hollow Trail": https://www.youtube.com/watch?v=H5QSiMUZ89k

Deborah Howard is a poet, and teacher of multilingual learners. She is the author of *Haiku 52: A Journey Through the Year in Poetry*. Her poems have appeared in journals including *Modern Haiku*, *Adanna*, and *cattails*.

The poem, "East Rock Park, 1978", was inspired by her husband's memories of growing up in New Haven in the 1970s.

Andy Horowitz is an Associate Professor of History at the University of Connecticut, and he serves as the Connecticut State Historian. His first book, *Katrina: A History, 1915–2015* (Harvard University Press), won the Bancroft Prize in American History. His writing has appeared in the *Washington Post, The Atlantic, Rolling Stone, Southern Cultures*, and *The New York Times*. He was born and raised in New Haven.

Jenevieve Carlyn Hughes: This poem emerged from the long hours spent with my mother while visiting a family member at Yale-New Haven Hospital, the same place I was born forty-three years ago. Our loved one has been fortunate to receive medical care there on many occasions, and this remains forefront even as we've searched for creative ways to lift our spirits during our visits. Despite the challenges, we treasure our shared memories, especially around the winter holidays.

Glinda Johnson-Medland was born and raised in Connecticut and spent much of her childhood in the woods and fields surrounding her home. She left Connecticut to attend college in Philadelphia and has remained in Pennsylvania for her adult career. With her husband Tom Johnson-Medland she co-authored *The Beauty of the Earth, Poems for the Child-Heart About the Planet.*

This poem is dedicated to my mom Gay Johnson and her sister Lynn Karolyi. They grew up in Gaylordsville and the New Milford area.

Marilyn E. Johnston has authored three poetry collections: *Downward Dreaming* (Grayson Books, 2023); *Weight of the Angel* and *Silk Fist Songs* (Antrim House) and a chapbook, *Against Disappearance*, Finalist in the 2001 Redgreene Press Poetry Prize. Her poems have appeared in numerous anthologies, and journals, such as *South Carolina Review, Poet Lore, bottle rockets, Worcester Review* and *The Wallace Stevens Journal*, garnering six Pushcart Prize nominations. She co-founded the popular Wintonbury Poetry Series in Bloomfield Public Library.

Megan Leonard: In 1692, Mercy Holbridge Disborough was accused of witchcraft, tried, and found guilty. This prose poem pulls heavily from the archived legal documents. Mercy was subjected to a "water test," which consisted of suspected witches being bound hand and foot and thrown into a body of water. If the accused witch sank, she was innocent. If she floated, it was evidence of her guilt. Mercy floated, and the fate of her trial was sealed.

John Long: I grew up in the Naugatuck River Valley near Torrington when family members and neighbors worked in the local factories. It was a time of stability and continuity. The entire community later experienced the destructive changes when those companies left Connecticut.

I lived on Hungerford Street in the mid-1970s when I wrote down some of the images and first fragmentary impressions. When I was much older, I discovered a way to develop a single poem that incorporated them. I think of "Hungerford Street" as a young man's observations combined with an old man's memories.

Katharyn Howd Machan: Born in Woodbury in 1952, I spent my early years in a house above Weekeepeemee Road. My grandmother often took me along on errands and visits, including travel into Roxbury to see an elderly friend. This woman on Tophet Road regularly connected with Marilyn Monroe, who lived nearby with her playwright husband. "Mrs. Miller," as the woman chose to call her, used to buy her groceries for her and help haul water from her well.

Marjorie Maddox: WPSU-FM *Poetry Moment* host, *Presence* assistant editor, and Professor Emerita at Commonwealth University, Marjorie Maddox has published 17 collections of poetry—including *Seeing Things, Hover Here, Small Earthly Space* and *In the Museum of My Daughter's Mind*—plus a story collection, five children's books, and the anthologies *Common Wealth: Contemporary Poets on Pennsylvania* and *Keystone Poetry* (co-editor). Her middle-grade biography, *A Man*

Named Branch: The True Story of Baseball's Great Experiment, is just out. www.marjoriemaddox.com

I often visit Mercy by the Sea Retreat Center in Madison, Connecticut. In that peaceful place, you'll find me walking the prayer labyrinth or on a bench mesmerized by the sea.

Pat Murphy McClelland is a poet currently living in Pasadena, California.

Melissa Dione McEwen: I wrote this poem while living with my boyfriend at the time and our young son on Center Street, just off Albany Avenue, across from the Citgo. The neighborhood gets a bad rep, but I've always been able to find the beauty in whatever place I call home. This poem came to me after watching a regular January afternoon—the boys on the corner, the buses rolling by like floats, the flamingo-pink sky over the Citgo, and it made the whole block feel briefly holy.

Mark McGuire-Schwartz strives to find a tad of originality in this world so overcrowded with words. This led to his creating a new poetic form, the Seventeen. His poem here is an example of that form. He is the Poet Laureate of Guilford, Connecticut.

This poem was inspired by the work of Milton Avery, by John Himmelfarb, Lee Krasner, Thomas Hart Benton, Adolf Gottlieb, Alexander Calder, and others, and by an overheard telephone conversation at the Rest Stop on 91.

Judith H. Montgomery's poems appear in *Poet Lore, Cider Press Review,* and *Epiphany,* among other journals, as well as in several anthologies. She's the author of two full-length poetry books and four chapbooks. Her first collection, *Passion,* received the Oregon Book Award for Poetry. Her prize-winning narrative medicine chapbook, *Mercy* (2019), was followed by *The Ferry Keeper,* which received the 2024 Grayson Books Chapbook Prize.

Pat Mottola teaches Creative Writing at Southern Connecticut State University, where she earned both an M.S. in Art Education and an M.F.A. in Creative Writing. An award-winning poet and Pushcart Prize nominee, her work is published in journals across the country. Mottola is President of the Connecticut Poetry Society and Poet Laureate of Cheshire, Connecticut. She served as editor of *Connecticut River Review* from 2012–2017. On a global scale, she mentors Afghan women writers living in Afghanistan and beyond. She is the author of three collections of poetry.

John Muro, a life-long resident of Connecticut, has authored three volumes of poems: In the *Lilac Hour* (2020), *Pastoral Suite* (2022) and *A Bountiful Silence* (2025). He has been nominated four times for the Pushcart Prize, two times for Best of the Net and he is also a Grantchester Award recipient. John's work has appeared in *Acumen*, *Belfast Review*, *Connecticut River*, *Sky Island*, the *Valparaiso Review* and elsewhere.

Tom Nicotera: Every year I try to go to Great Pond State Forest in Simsbury on Thanksgiving Day. I find that in this place of serenity and grace there are many natural phenomena to be thankful for, and I especially give thanks that the state has decided to preserve this gem of the natural world.

Victoria Nordgren: The Connecticut Sound Shore at Greenwich Point is the location for "Towards Greenwich Point." Section two contains a brief history of the remarkable woman who was a founder of Greenwich. She was one of the first women to own land in her own name. What was once her land is now a stunningly beautiful public park and a unique environment full of wildlife.

Julia Paul is author of two full-length collections, *Shook*, (Grayson Books) and *Table with Burning Candle*, (Cornerstone Press) and a chapbook, *Staring Down the Tracks* (The Poetry Box). Her poems are widely published in journals and anthologies. Her poem, *Dear Coroner, How Could You Know*, appears in the 2023 *Pushcart Prize Best of the*

Small Presses anthology. Paul leads the Riverwood Poetry Series in Hartford, Connecticut. She is an elder law attorney in Manchester, Connecticut.

Garrett Phelan: *Confirmation* and *The Chrome Plating Line at Pratt & Whitney* are two poems focused on a teenager growing up in the 1960s. *Confirmation* expresses the edgy freedom of an early teen just as adulthood begins to challenge that freedom. *The Chrome Plating Line at Pratt & Whitney* is of an older teen at a moment when a summer job changes the course of his life.

Elizaberh Poliner: I wrote this poem while teaching a creative writing class. One day we focused on bells, and I recalled the lack of bells in our town, once known as "Belltown," for manufacturing bells. My books include the poetry collection, *What You Know in Your Hands* (David Robert Books), and the novels *As Close to Us as Breathing* (Little Brown & Co.) and *Spinning at the Edges* (Harper)—all books with lots of Connecticut in them.

Geri Radacsi is the author of four collections of poetry and a soon to be released collection, 24-Hours of Savage Amusement. Among her publications are the prize-winning chapbook, *Ancient Music*, and her full-length poetry collections: *Trapped in Amber*, *Tightrope Walker Soul and All that Jazz* and *The Oarsman*. She has been a journalist, English teacher, communication/media specialist, and freelance writer. Currently, she is Associate Director of University Relations, Emerita, at Central Connecticut State University in New Britain, Connecticut.

Charles Rafferty has published poems in such places as *The New Yorker*, *Ploughshares*, and *The Southern Review*. His most recent collection is *The Appendectomy Grin* (BOA Editions). He is also the author of the poetry chapbook *The Problem With Abundance*, the story collection *Somebody Who Knows Somebody*, and the novel *Moscodelphia*.

Gwen North Reiss's poem "Willow" was awarded the 2025 Nutmeg Prize from the Connecticut Poetry Society. "Louis Kahn," included here, focuses on the Yale Center for British Art, though it speaks more broadly of Kahn's work, which included his first major public commission, the Yale University Art Gallery—across the street. Her poem "West Rock" is an attempt to capture the geology and stark beauty of that ridge.

Bessy Reyna has served as Bolton Poet Laureate for several years. Her poetry chapbooks include *Memoirs of the Unfaithful Lover/Memorias de la amante infiel; She Remembers* and *Battlefield of Your Body*. Her work has been included in numerous anthologies, and she has participated in international poetry festivals in Latin America. Her advocacy in support of artists and the Latino community was recognized with the awards of "Latina Citizen of the Year" and American Association of Hispanics in Higher Education, among several others. www.bessyreyna.com

C.M. Rivers grew up reading stacks of books to the sound of rain on the roof in Oregon's Willamette Valley. The author of two award-winning books of poetry, his work has appeared in literary magazines across the United States. He lives in California. www.cmrivers.com

Eva M. Schlesinger grew up hiking, biking, swimming, and playing in Southeastern Connecticut. Recipient of the Literal Latté Food Verse Award, her titles include *Remembering the Walker & Wheelchair: poems of grief and healing* (Finishing Line Press, 2008) and *View From My Banilla Vanilla Villa* (dancing girl press, 2010). Schlesinger is working on a short fiction collection and YA novel, except when she's visiting her favorite areas or eating grinders and pizza in Connecticut.

Natalie Schriefer is an academic editor and freelance writer. When she isn't at her desk, she's often out walking or learning a new sport.

Over eight years, I drafted close to 50 different versions of "At Connecticut River Motocross." Each version felt incomplete until I eventually expanded it—the inclusion of more track details gave the poem a wider context and helped it feel, finally, complete.

Sara Shea received her BA from Kenyon College, where she served as Student Associate Editor for The Kenyon Review. She's pursued graduate studies through the Great Smokies Writing Program at UNC Asheville and at Western Carolina University, where she studied with Ron Rash. Shea is the recipient of numerous awards and fellowships, including the New Millennium Poetry Prize judged by UK Poet Laureate Andrew Motion. Shea writes professionally, producing marketing materials for a fine arts gallery in Asheville, North Carolina.

Vivian Shipley's 14th full-length book of poetry is *Slow Dancing with the Dark* (Louisiana Literature Press, SLU, 2024). *Hindsight: 2020* (Louisiana Literature Press, SLU, 2022) was awarded the 2023 Paterson Poetry Prize for Literary Excellence. Previous books have won New England Poetry Club's Sheila Motton Award, the Word Press Poetry Prize, Library of Congress' CT Center for the Book Poetry Prize twice, and a Housatonic CT Book Award. Shipley is the CSU Distinguished Professor, Emeritus. She has a PhD from Vanderbilt University and was inducted into UK's Hall of Distinguished Alumni. Vivianshipley.net

Julia Meylor Simpson: I worked part-time at the wonderful Lyman Allyn Art Museum in New London for more than five years when I retired from a career in corporate communications in Rhode Island and moved to Connecticut. After spending a lifetime writing and teaching for a living, it was a joy to be surrounded by galleries of artwork and sculptures. I hope this poem honors the work done there to celebrate the arts.

Sharon Smith: We live in Farmington, Connecticut, right across the street from a town forest. We are frequently visited by bears, squirrels, birds, chipmunks, earthworms, bees, frogs, turtles and the occasional deer.

John Stanizzi is the author of *Pond, See*, and 11 other titles. His poems have appeared in *Prairie Schooner, Cortland Review, Rattle*, among other publications.

Regarding "New Autumn:" It's late September. A butterfly, the poem's heart, slowed by new coolness, works its wings gently, uniformly, praising fall's spectacular opening act. I recall it with perfect resolution.

Melissa Studdard writes poetry, song cycles, and libretti, and is the author of six books. Her most recent poetry collection, *Dear Selection Committee*, includes poems featured by *The New York Times, The Penn Review Poetry Prize*, the *Best American Poetry* blog, and the Lucille Medwick Award for the Poetry Society of America. Her writing has also been featured by outlets such as *The Guardian, Ms. Magazine*, PBS, and NPR.

Steve Straight's books include *Affirmation* (Grayson Books, 2022), which won the 2023 William Meredith Award for Poetry, *The Almanac* (Curbstone/Northwestern University Press, 2012) and *The Water Carrier* (Curbstone, 2002). He was professor of English and director of the poetry program at Manchester Community College, in Connecticut.

Maxine Susman writes about human and more-than-human worlds, art, and history. She has published eight poetry collections and teaches poetry writing at the Osher Lifelong Learning Institute of Rutgers University.

The Florence Griswold Museum, a National Historic Site, has beautiful grounds and gardens, a modern gallery, and tours of the boardinghouse run by resourceful Florence Griswold, a sea captain's daughter who made an unusual contribution to American art.

Elizabeth Thomas is a published writer and performer who designs and teaches creative writing and oral history programs for all ages. These programs promote literacy and the power of written and spoken word.

Her current focus is helping to build writing communities among older adults. She believes poetry is meant to be heard out loud and in person.

Sue Ellen Thompson is the author of six books of poetry—most recently *Sea Nettles: New & Selected Poems*. She has taught at Middlebury College, Binghamton University, Wesleyan University, Central Connecticut State University, and the University of Delaware. A resident of Oxford, Maryland since 2006, she mentors adult poets and teaches workshops at The Writer's Center in Washington, D.C. In 2010, the Maryland Library Association awarded her its prestigious Maryland Author Award.

Steve Veilleux lives in northeastern Connecticut. He's inspired by the magical beauty of his remote environment. His poetry has appeared in various anthologies, including *Silkworm, Connecticut Bards Poetry Review, Many Voices – One Stage*. His first poetry book is *Event Horizon*, and he is currently working on a second, *What the Moleman Said*. I grew up looking at the tobacco fields near the Farmington River, fell from canoes along its rapids, camped for years on the shore of Long Island Sound.

Terri Yannetti is a Milford-based newspaper writer. Her poetry has appeared or is forthcoming in *Asimov's, The Magazine of Fantasy & Science Fiction* and *Star*Line*.

Sandra Yannone, Poet Laureate of Old Saybrook, published *The Glass Studio* (2024) and *Boats for Women* (2019) with Salmon Poetry in County Clare, Ireland. Her father, stained glass artist Vincent Yannone (1936-2022), survived the Hartford Circus Fire of 1944 depicted in her poem. She is the co-editor of the forthcoming anthology *Unsinkable: Poetry Inspired by the Titanic* (Salmon, 2026). MoonPath Press will publish her chapbook, *Fire at the Big Top*, in late spring, 2026.

Elaine Zimmerman: I wrote *The Guest* after television coverage of this bear crashing a toddler's party in West Hartford. The bear enjoyed the party, gobbling down cupcakes at a picnic table. Bear was too relaxed, while the children were both excited and startled. It was a moment that highlighted environmental change and our youngest generation experiencing the outcomes. I tried to imagine the birthday boy's insights and feelings.

Permission Credits

Chris Abbate: "Home Run" first appeared in *Connecticut River Review*.

Elizabeth Alexander: "Allegiance," © by Elizabeth Alexander and co-authored with Marilyn Nelson, was first published in *Miss Crandall's School for Young Ladies and Little Misses of Color*, (2007), Wordsong.

Sherri Bedingfield: "Conversation with White Rose" was first published in *Where Flowers Bloom: Poems of Elizabeth Park* (Ginny Lowe Connors, ed.), Grayson Books.

Sarah Blanchard: "Woodstock in Stones" first appeared in *river, horse, morning*, Eagle Ridge Press.

Ginny Lowe Connors: "The Mark Twain House" first appeared in *Of Hartford in Many Lights: Celebrating Hartford's Buildings* (Dennis Barone & Deborah Ducoff-Barone, eds.), Grayson Books.

Robert Cording: "For a Friend's Baby" was first published in *Orion*.

Brad Davis: "On the Way to Putnam" first appeared in Poetry.

Cortney Davis: "This Is a Poem About Snow" first appeared in *The Healing Muse, Vol.24, No.1*.

Tony Fusco: "Allingtown" and "The Last Day of School" first appeared in *Jessie's Garden*, Negative Capability Press.

Natasha S. Garnett: "After the Hurricane" was originally published in *Toasted Cheese Literary Journal*.

Margaret Gibson: (Flood Plain, Lit and Shadowed by Sun and Clouds" was first published in *Writing the Land: Currents* (L. McLoughlin, ed.).

Anne Hampford: "First Snow" was originally published in *Voices Elevated: 10 Years of the Elk River Writers Workshop*.

Dolores Hayden: "In the Middle Lane, Leaving New Haven" was first published in *The Yale Review*.

Ruth Hoberman: "In Abeyance" was first published in *Connecticut River Review*.

Joan Hofmann: "At Powder Hollow Trail" first appeared in *Writing the Land: The Connecticut River* (Lis McLoughlin, ed.), NatureCulture.

Jenevieve Carlyn Hughes: "Sanctuary" was first published in *Black Bough Poetry's Christmas & Winter Anthology, Volume 6*.
John Long: "Industrial Heartland" first appeared in *Here: a poetry journal*.

Katharyn Howd Machan: "Roxbury, 1956" first appeared in *The MacGuffin, 24, No. 2*.

Melissa Dione McEwen: "Sketch of Albany Ave. in the Afternoon, Late January" was originally published in *hashtagartmag*.

Judith Montgomery: "Eden" was first published in *Vermont Literary Review*.

John Muro: "Overwintering" was first published in *Belladonna's Garden Literary Magazine*.

Garrett Phelan: "The Chrome Plating Line at Pratt & Whitney" *was first published in Off the Coast. "Confirmation" first appeared in The Courtship of Winds*.

Elizabeth Poliner: "East Hampton, Connecticut 1977" was first published in *Seneca Review*.

Charles Rafferty: "Newtown" was originally published in *The Appendectomy Grin*, BOA Editions.

C.M. Rivers: "Last Supper" first appeared in *Connecticut River Review*.

Eva M. Schlesinger: "Remembering a Connecticut Childhood" was first published in *Awake in the World, V.II*, Riverfeet Press.

Natalie Schriefer: "At Connecticut River Motocross" first appeared in *Room Magazine, Issue 42.3*.

Vivian Shipley: "Frances Splettstocher, 21" was first published in *All of Your Messages Have Been Erased*, Louisiana Literature Press, Southeastern Louisiana University. "May 25, 1647, Gov. John Winthrop Recorded the First Execution for Witchcraft in the New World: [   ] of Windsor, Connecticut" first appeared in *Hindsight 2020*, Louisiana Literature Press, Southeastern Louisiana University.

Steve Straight: "Old Longtooth" was first published in *Connecticut River Review*.

Maxine Susman: "Florence Griswold's Boardinghouse" was first published in *Northern Swim*, Ragged Sky Press.

Sue Ellen Thompson: "Connecticut in March" was first published in *The Leaving: New & Selected Poems*, Autumn House Press.

Sandra Yannone: "The Ten Worst Fires in U.S. History" was first published in *ABQ in Print, #9*.

Elaine Zimmerman: "The Guest" was first published in *Oberon Poetry, Twenty Second Annual Issue, 2024* (Mindy Kronenberg, ed.), Oberon Foundation.